Spiritual
COLORING BOOK

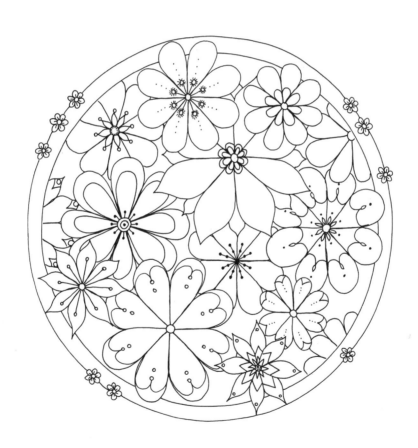

Spiritual
COLORING BOOK

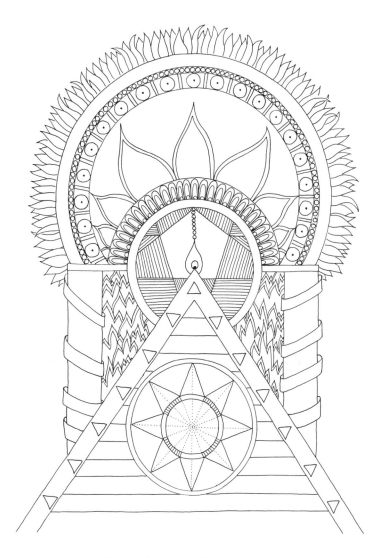

Andrea Sargent

CHARTWELL
BOOKS

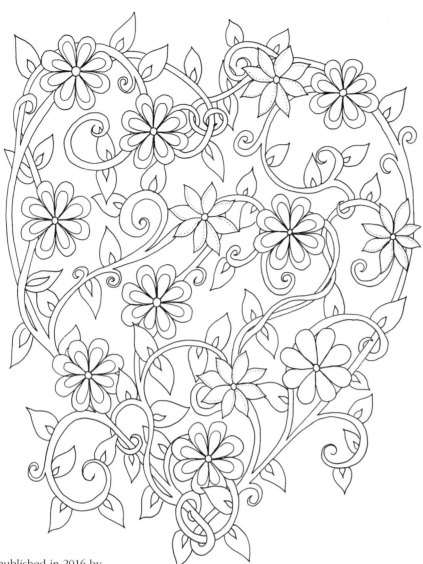

This edition published in 2016 by
CHARTWELL BOOKS
an imprint of Book Sales
a division of Quarto Publishing Group USA Inc.
142 West 36th Street, 4th Floor
New York, New York 10018
USA

ISBN: 978-0-7858-3417-5
CH004963NT

Cover Design: Maki Ryan

Printed in China

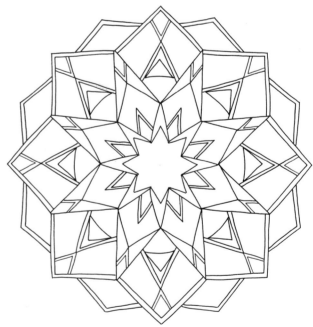

INTRODUCTION

These images for coloring are inspired by spiritual and religious iconography. They are specifically designed to promote a sense of calm, so that you can focus your mind on creativity. Hopefully you will enjoy selecting from a range of colors and media and experimenting with different styles for your coloring. You can use block coloring, blending, layering, shading, highlighting—there are so many possibilities!

I have drawn all the images by hand in black ink. They vary in complexity and abstractness; some may take a few days to complete, others can be done during your lunch hour or in the evening with a cup of cocoa.

I hope you derive a sense of well-being from coloring these pages. For more coloring happiness, find me on facebook: www.facebook.com/thehappyoctopusart or instagram: www.instagram.com/thehappyoctopusart. And send me the results—I would love to see your completed pictures!

Andrea Sargent

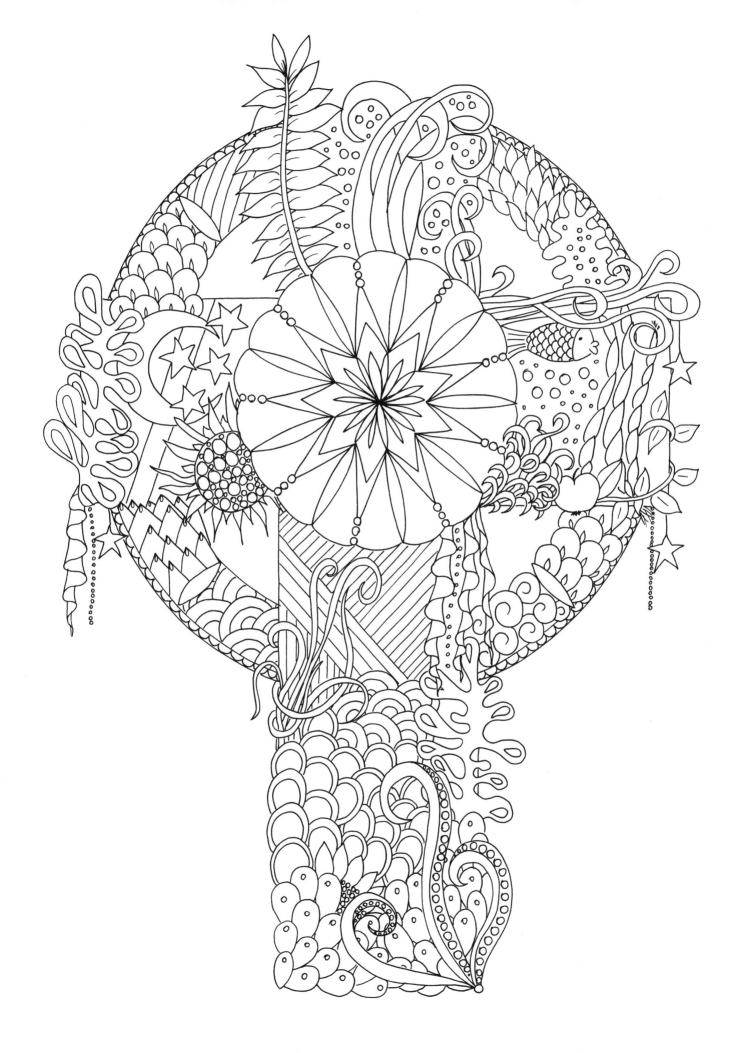

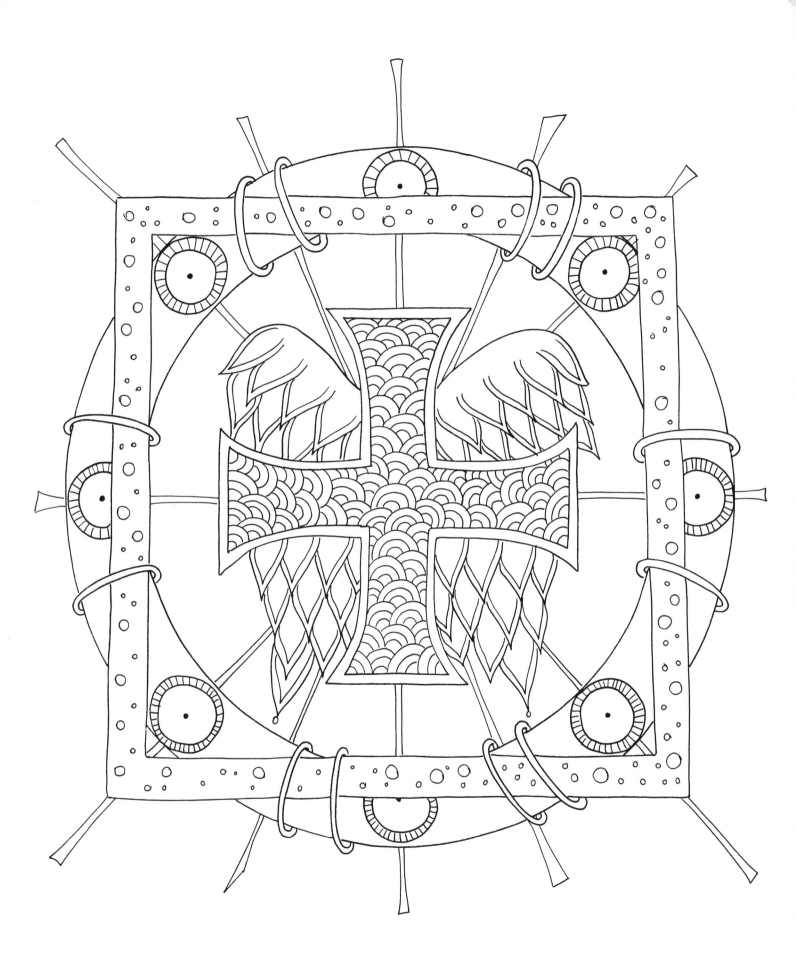

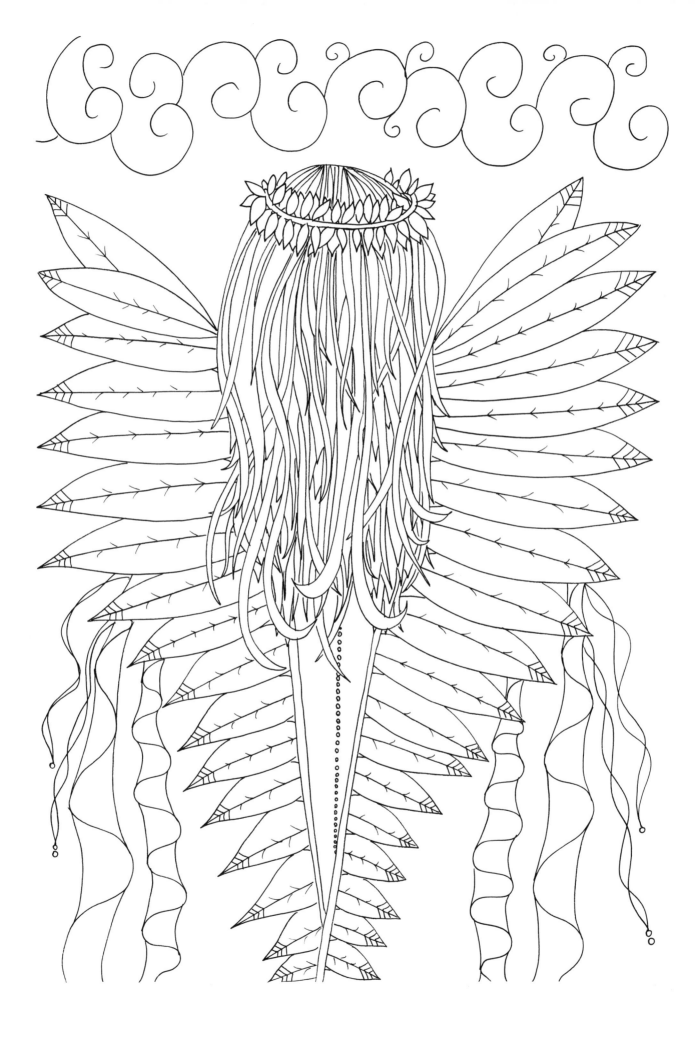

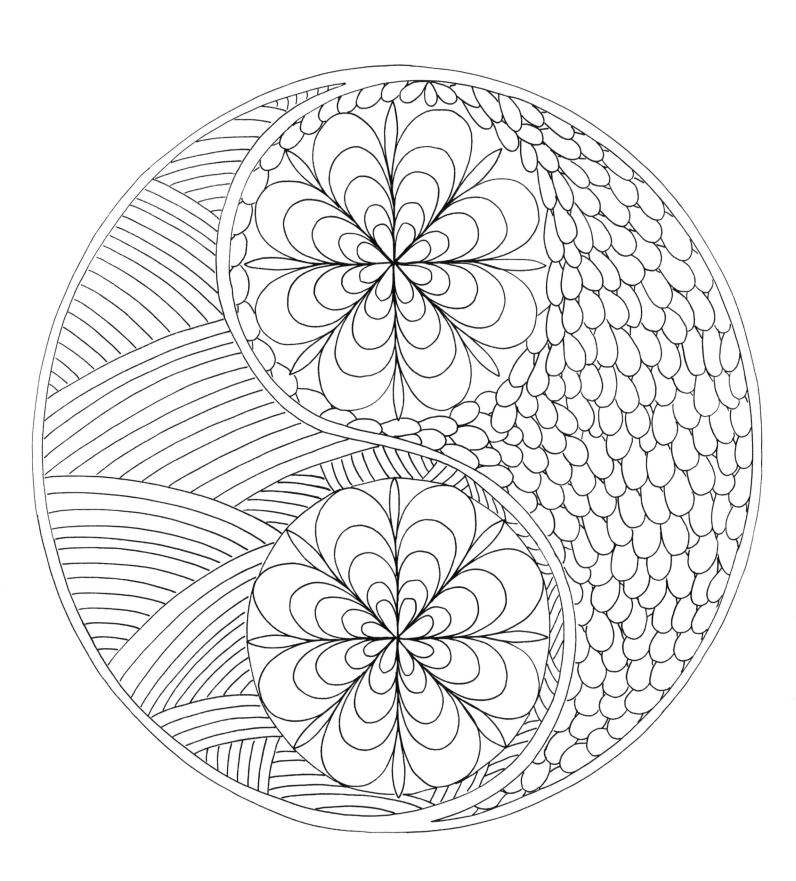

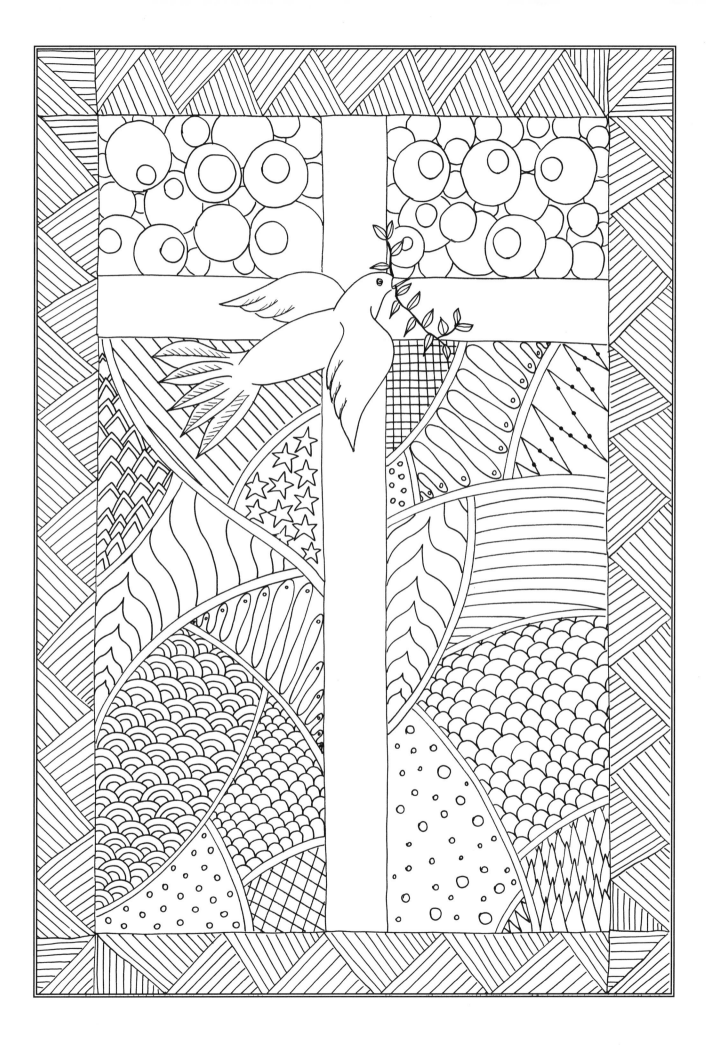

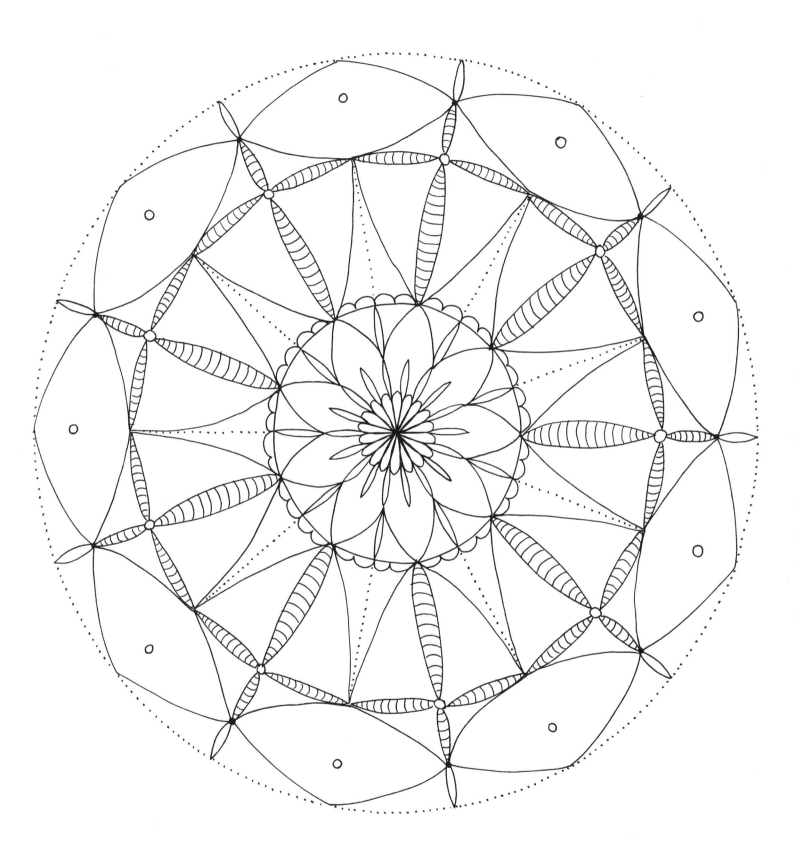

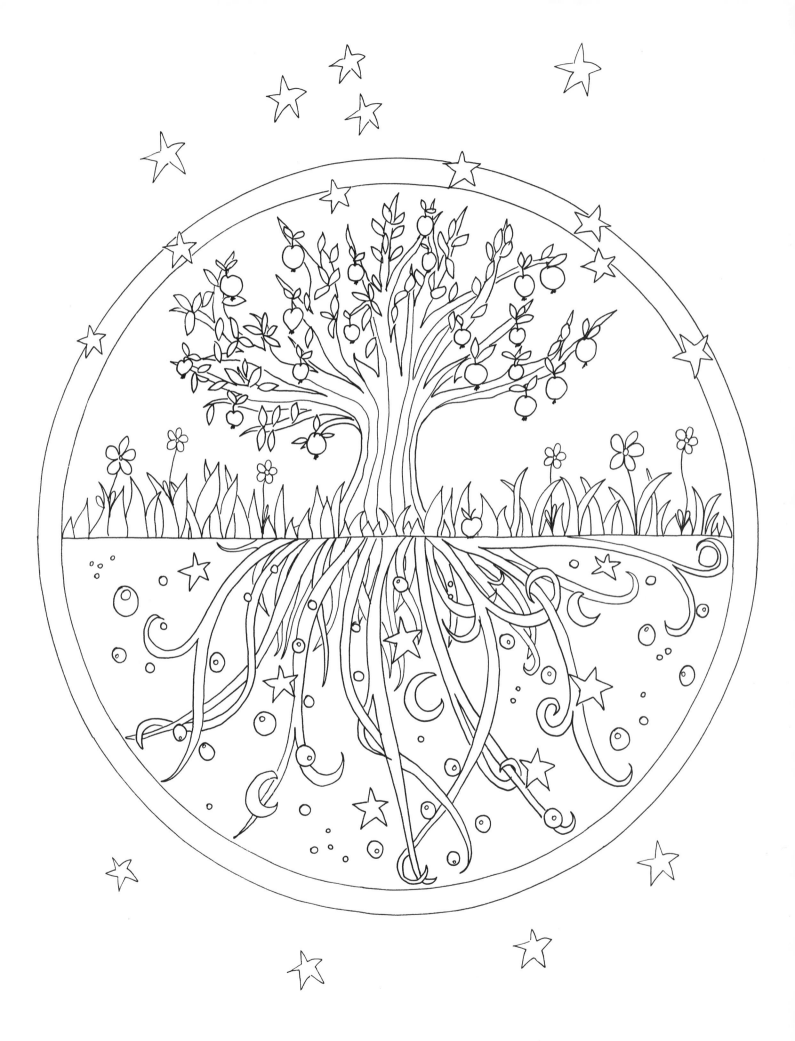

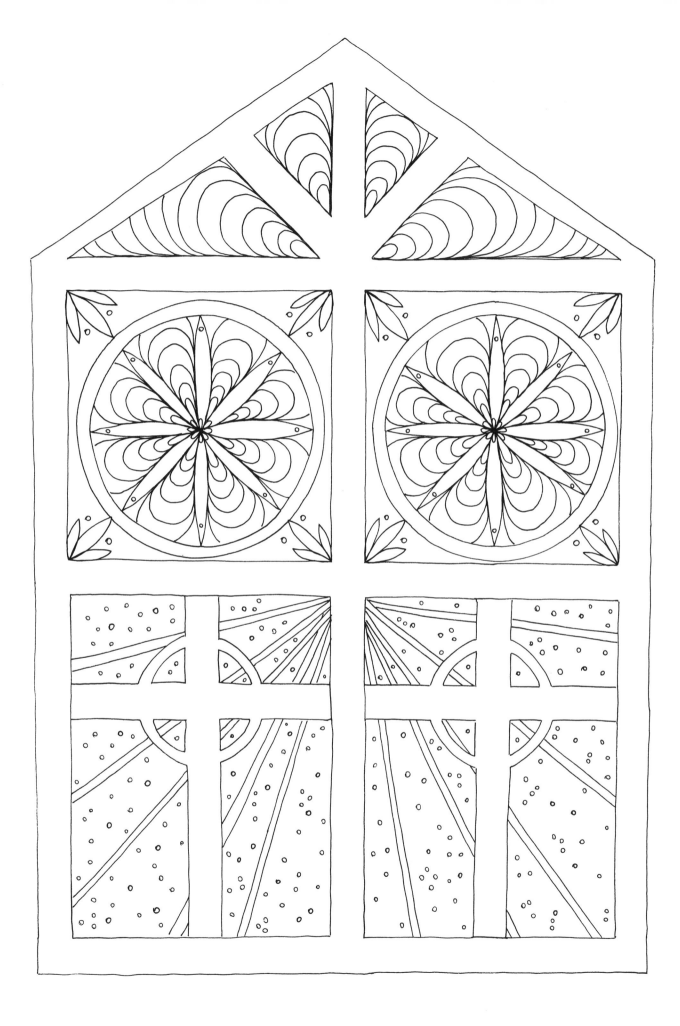

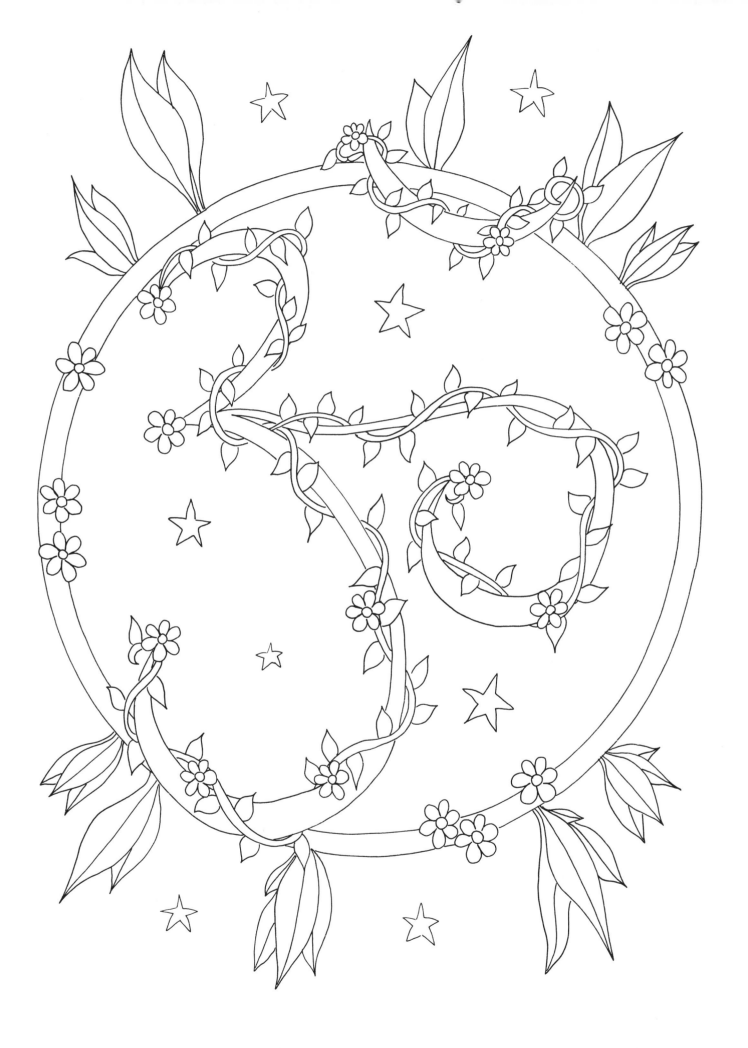

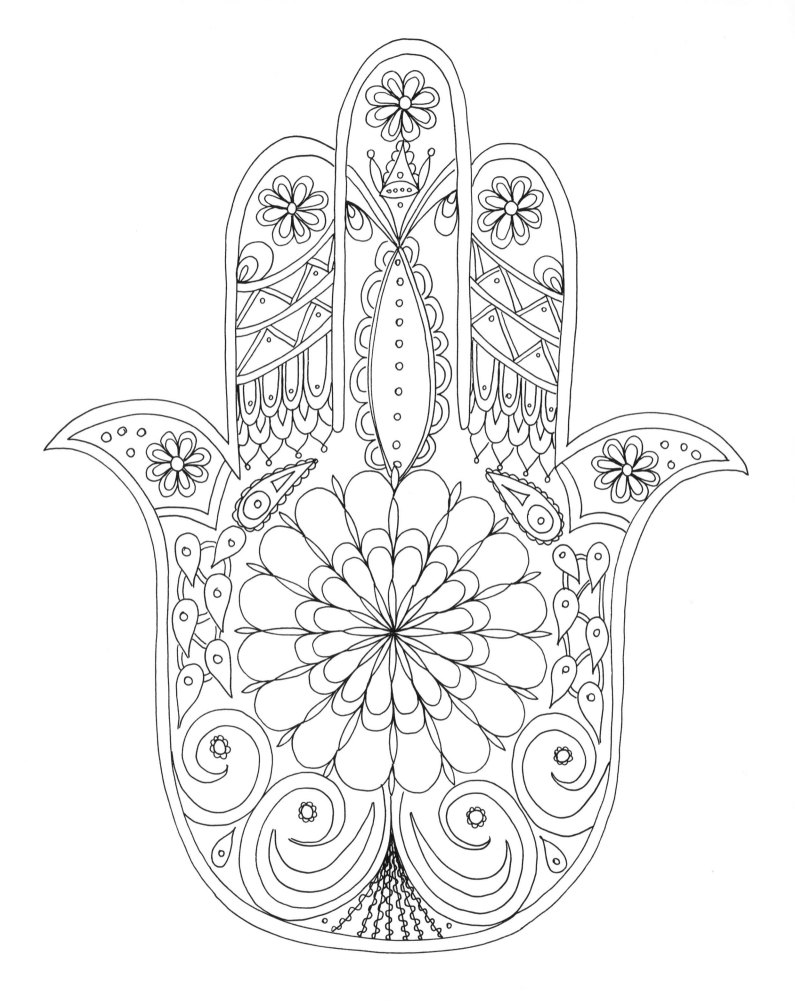

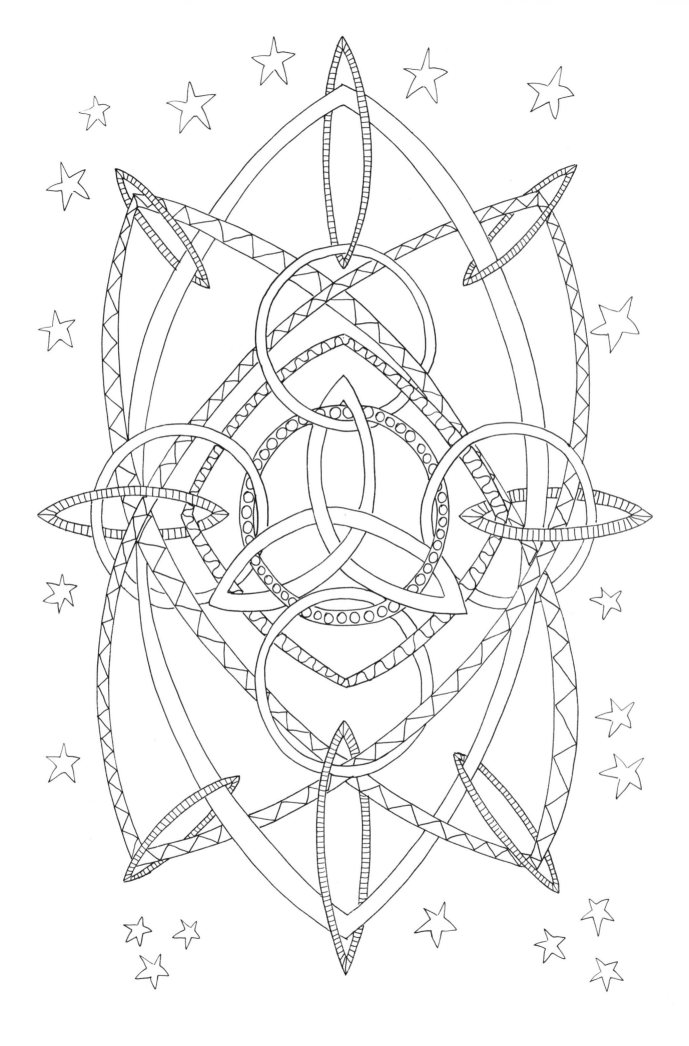

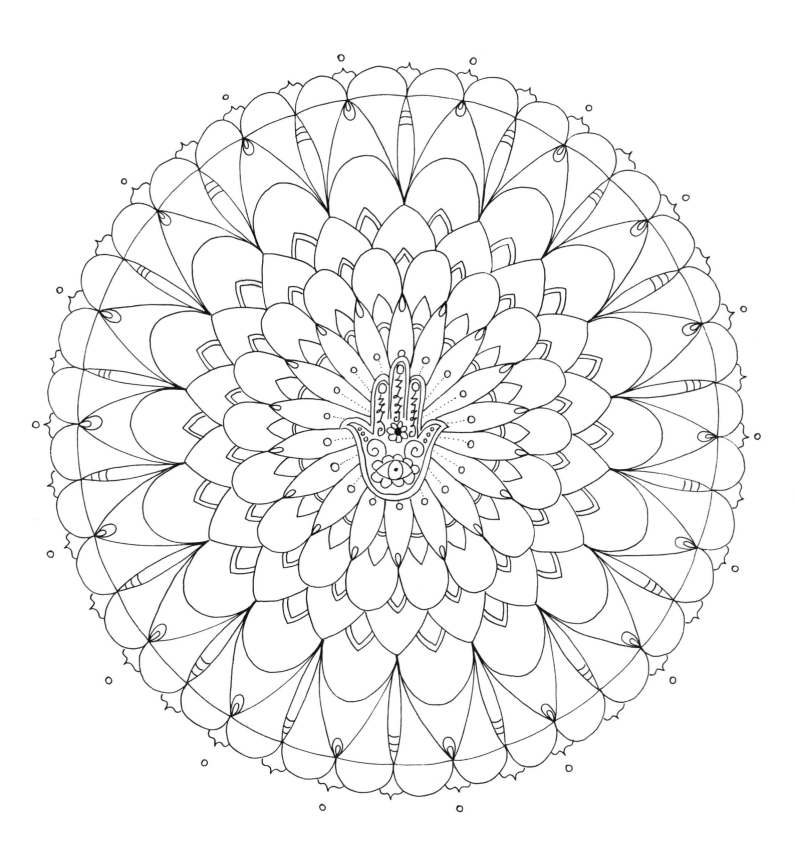

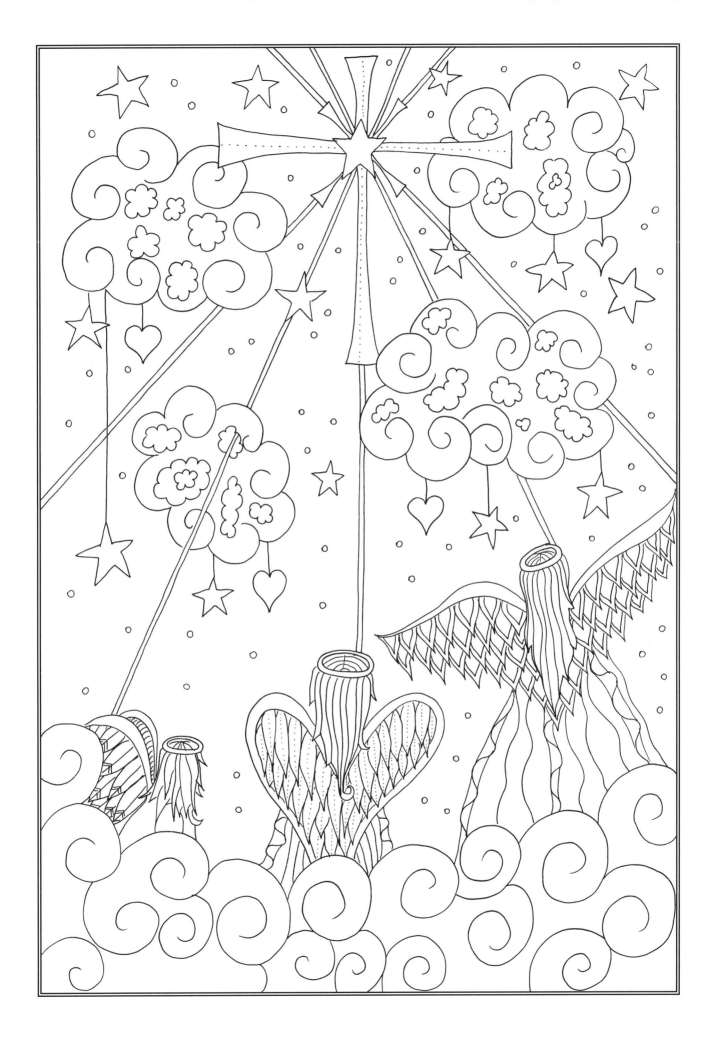

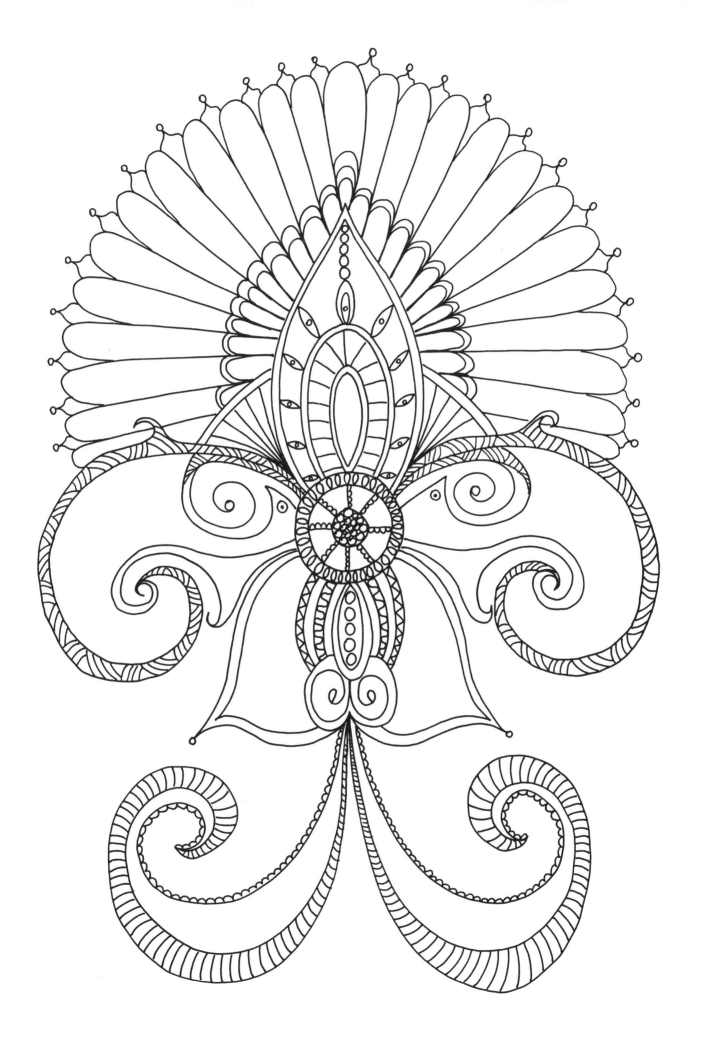

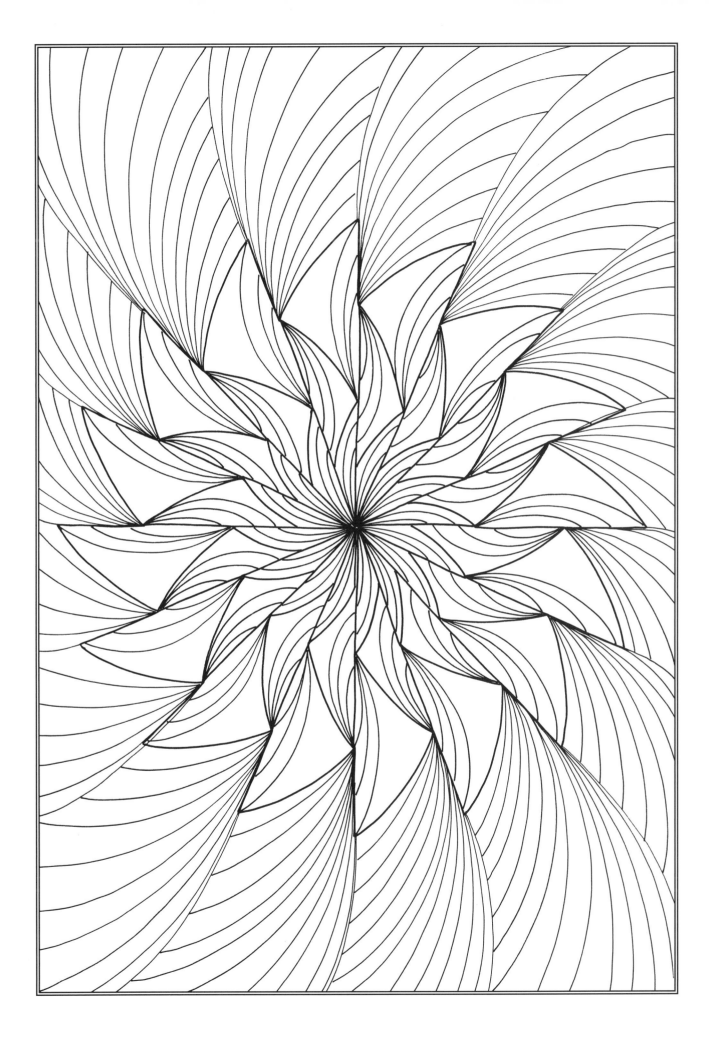

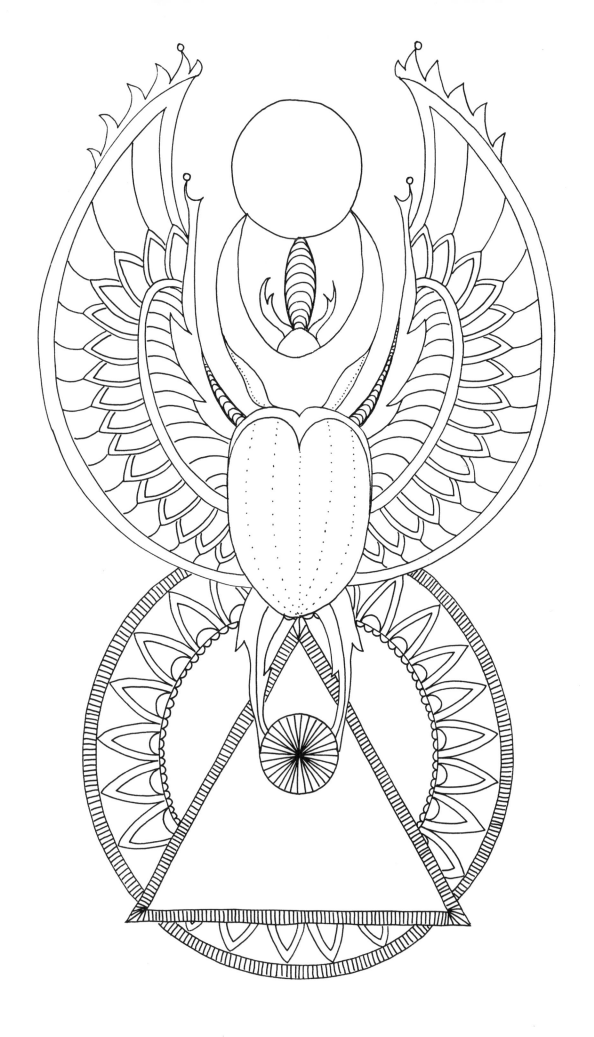

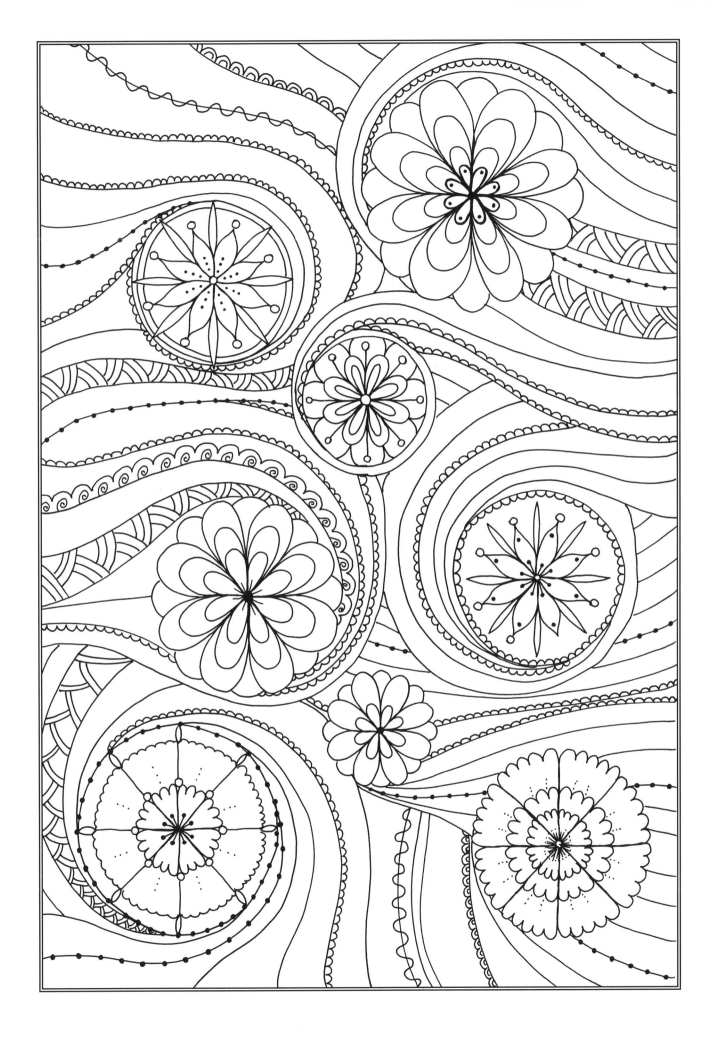

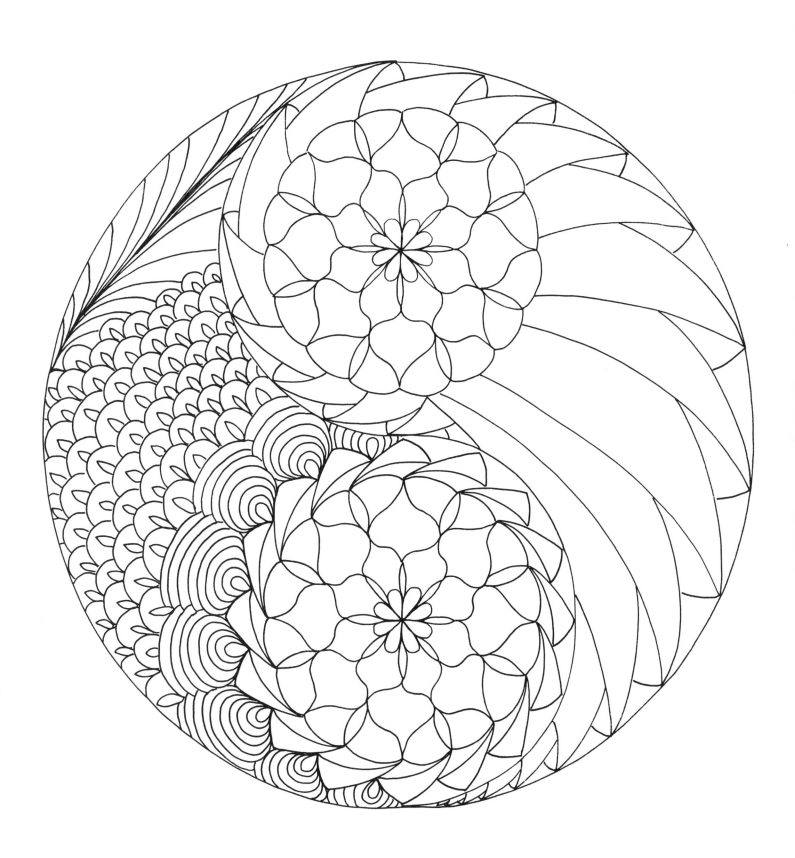

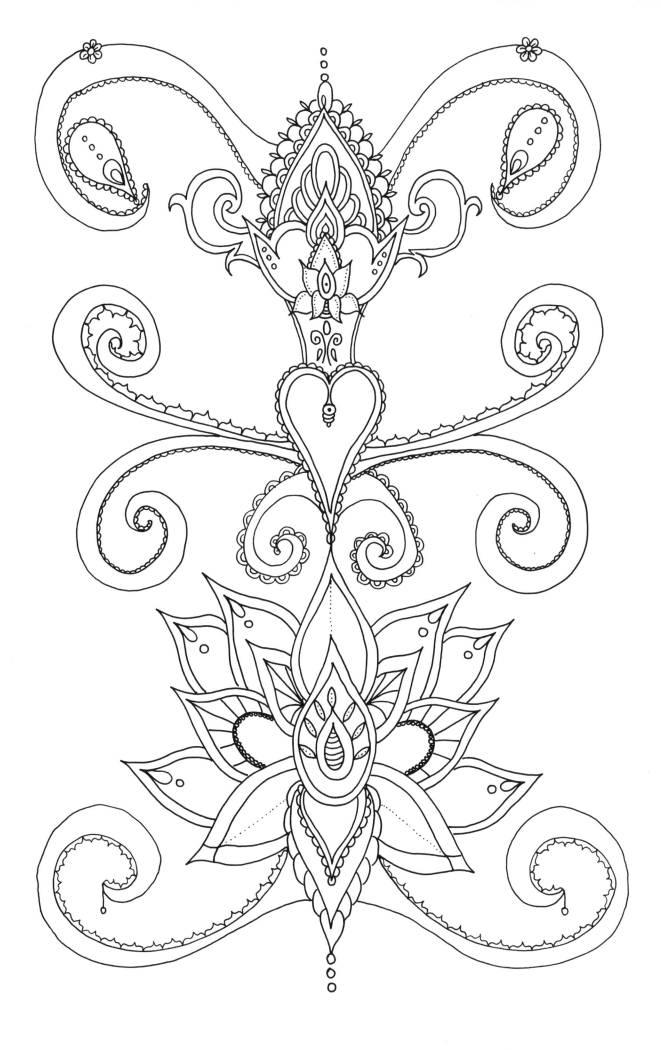

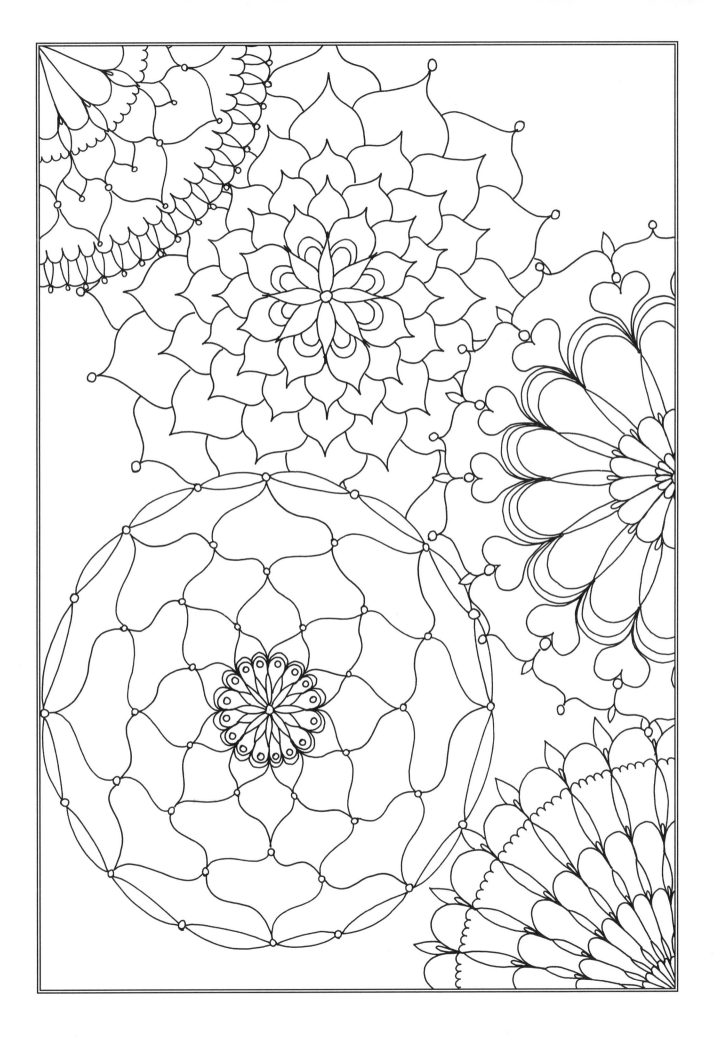

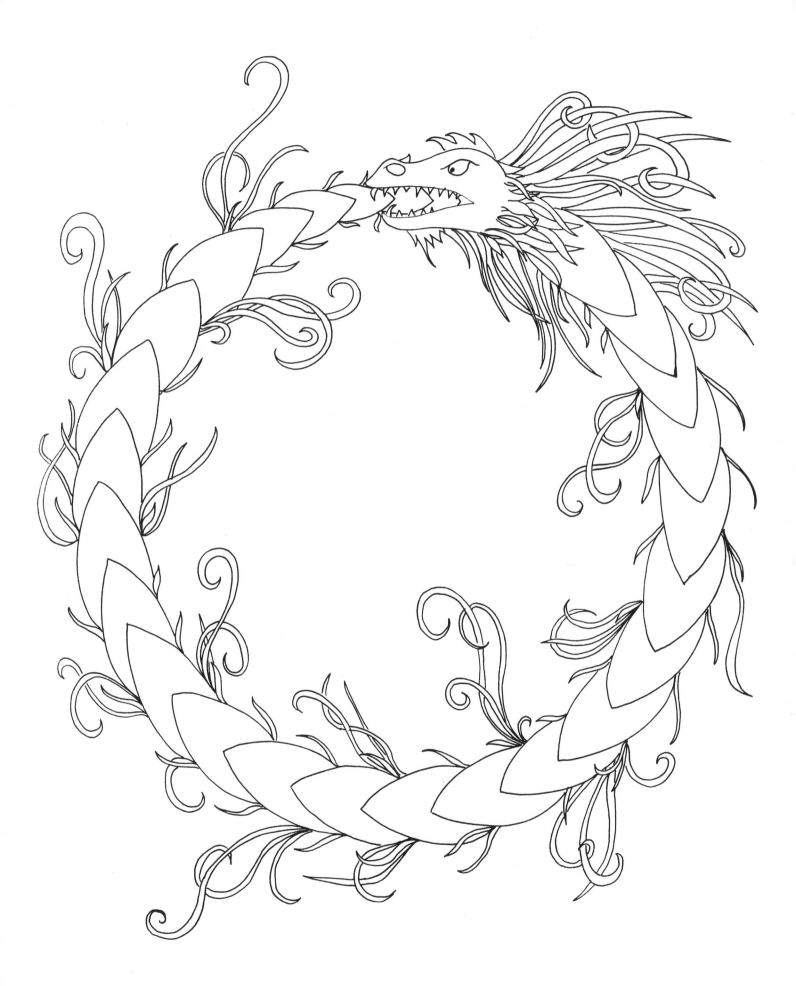

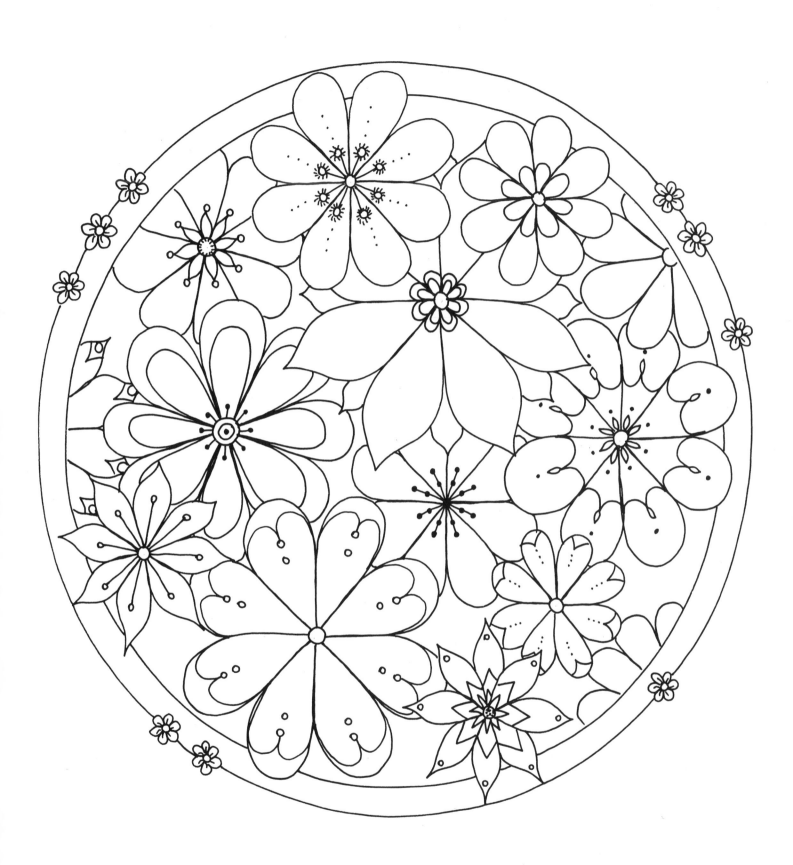

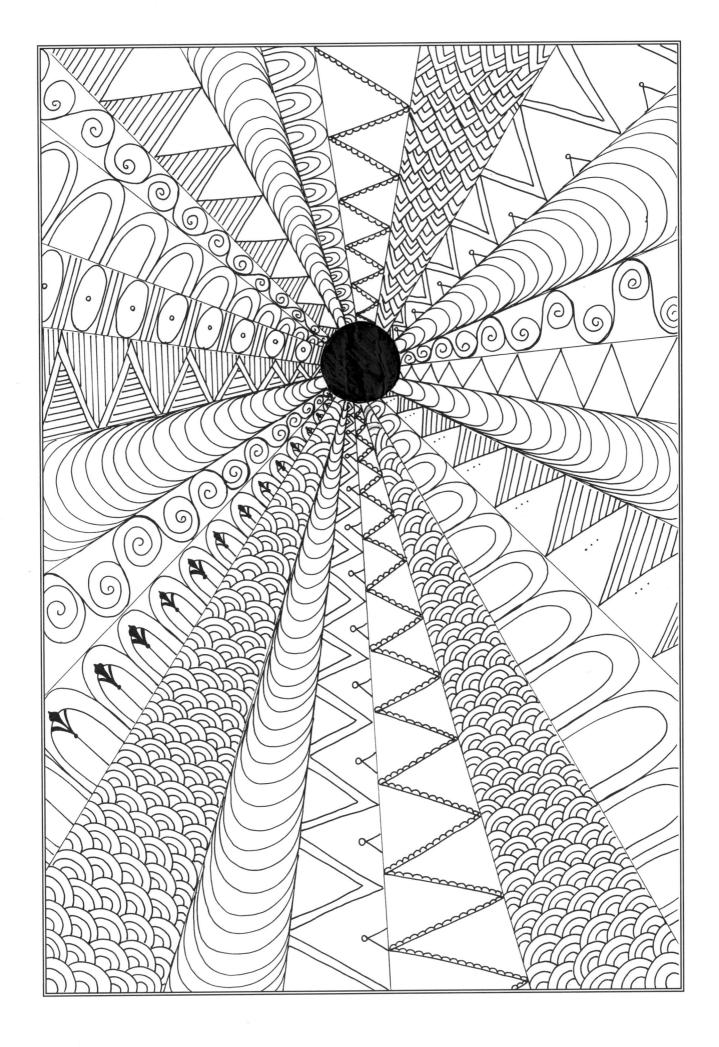

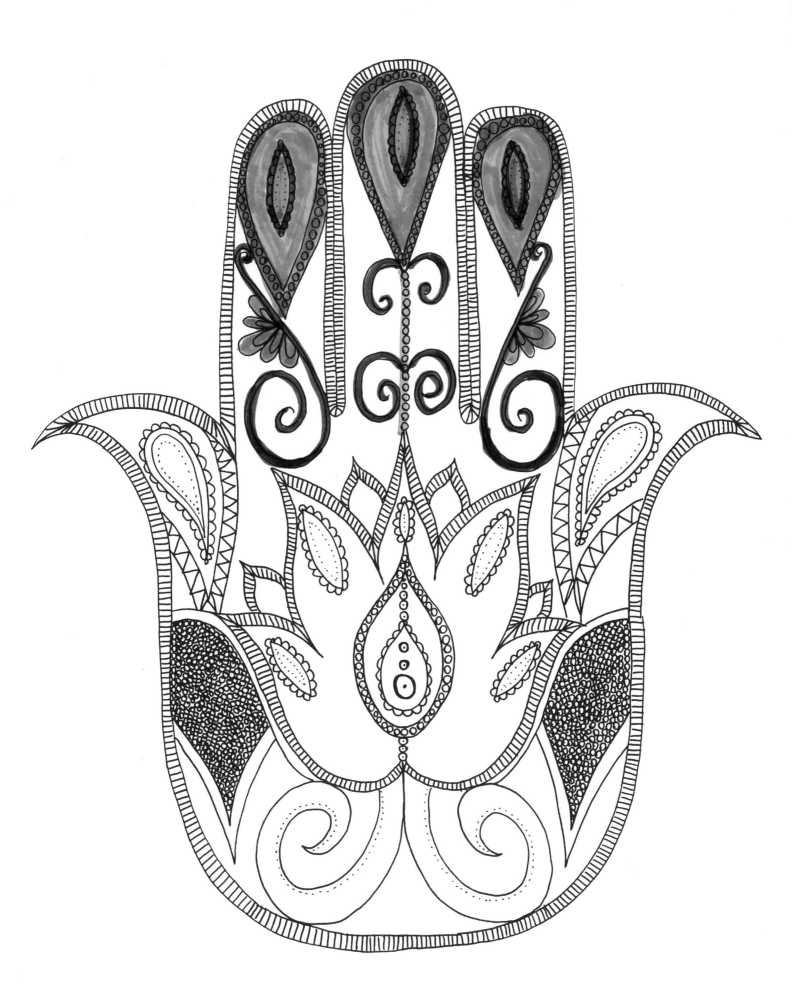

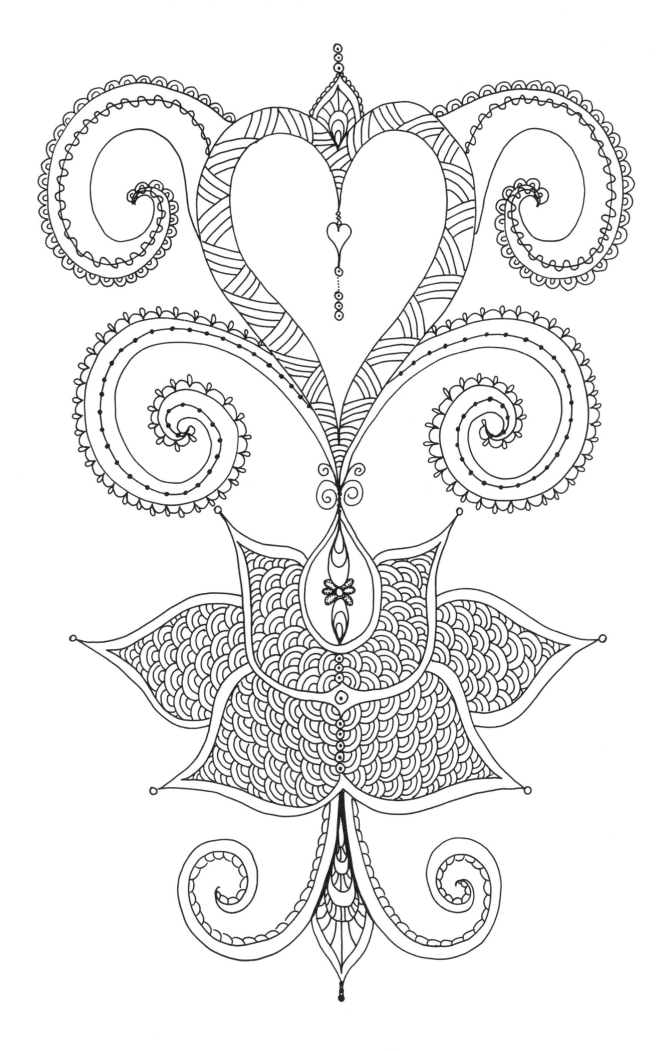

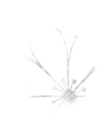

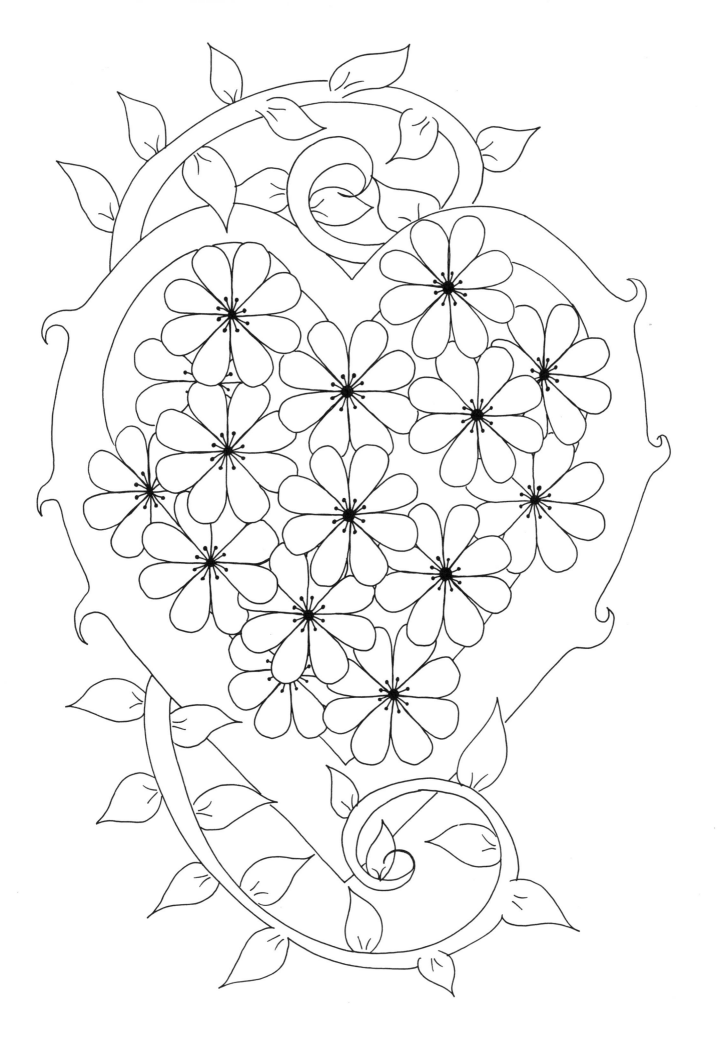

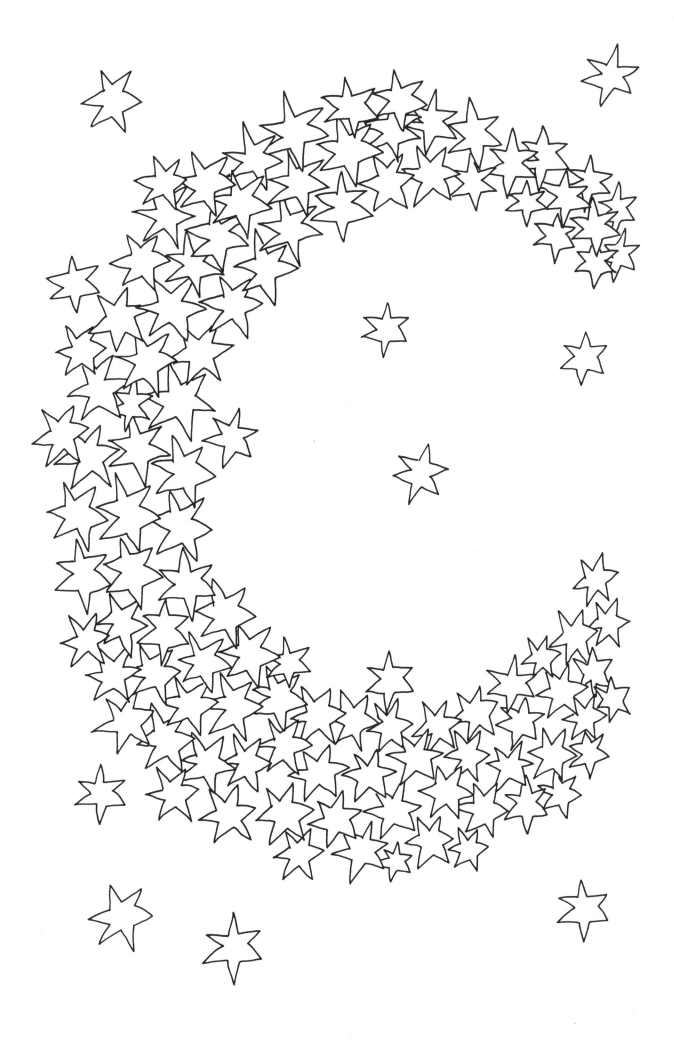

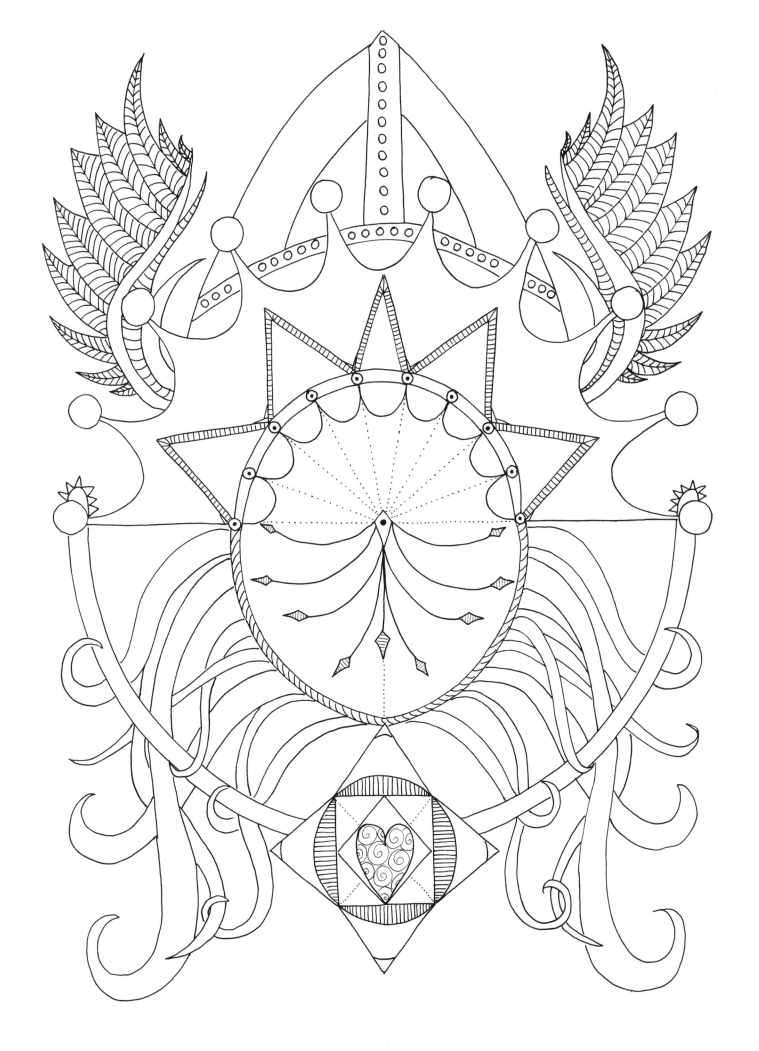

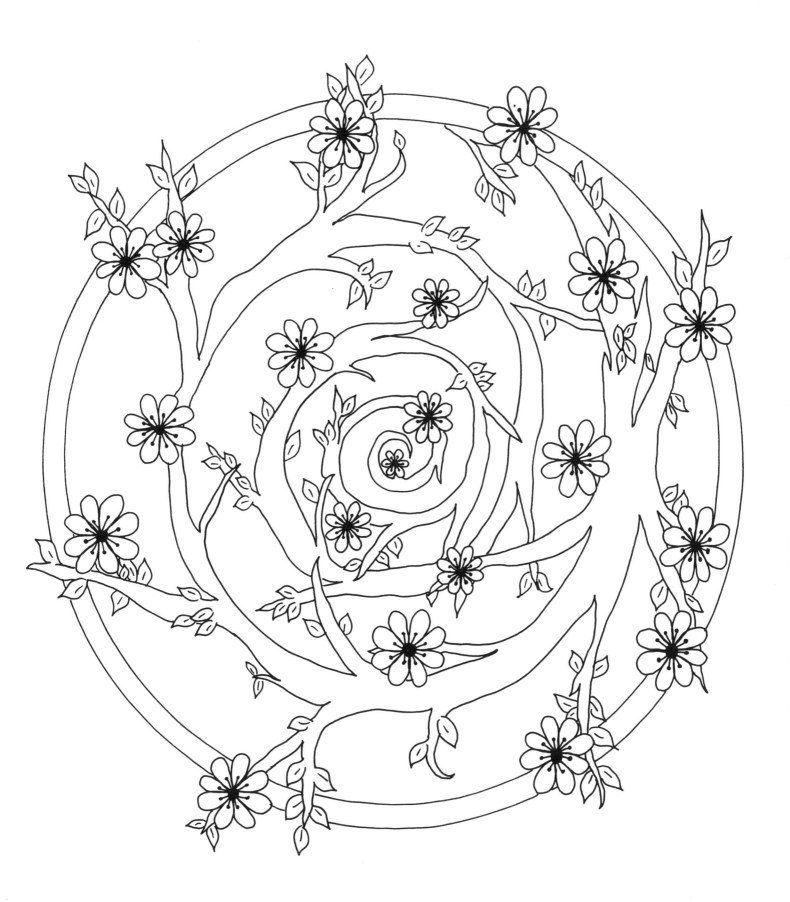

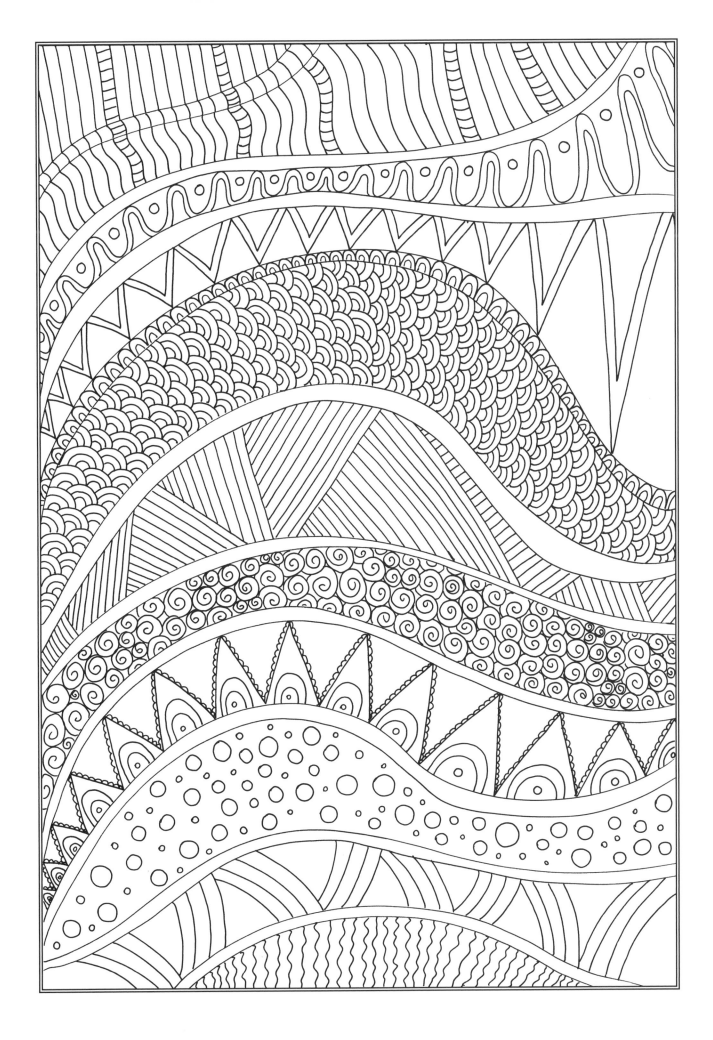

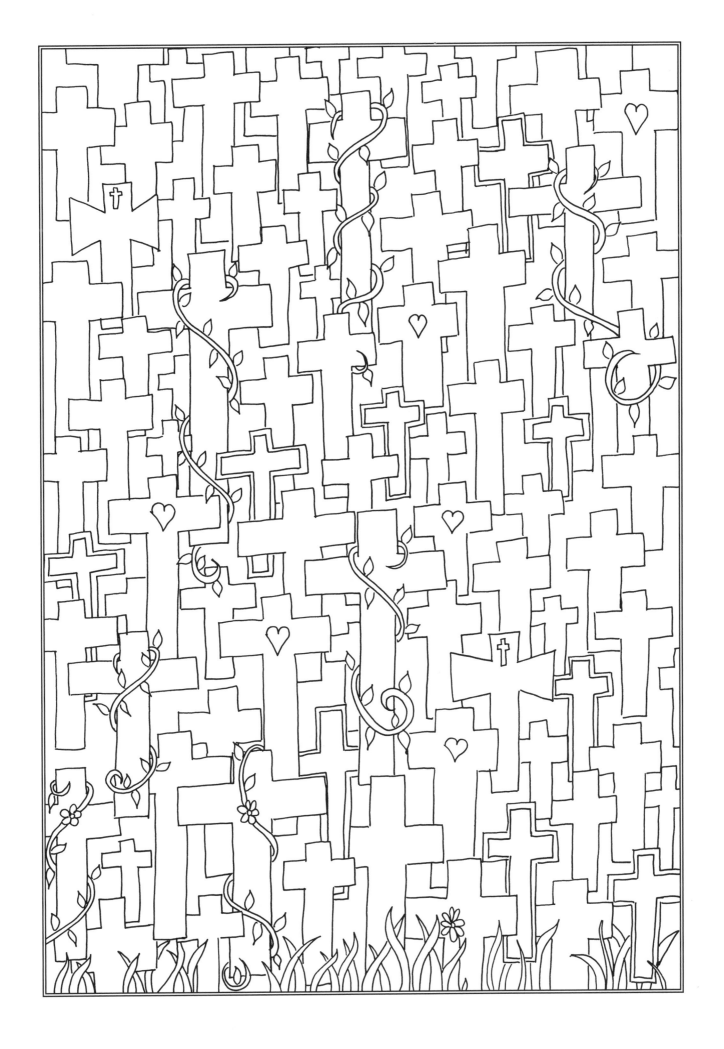

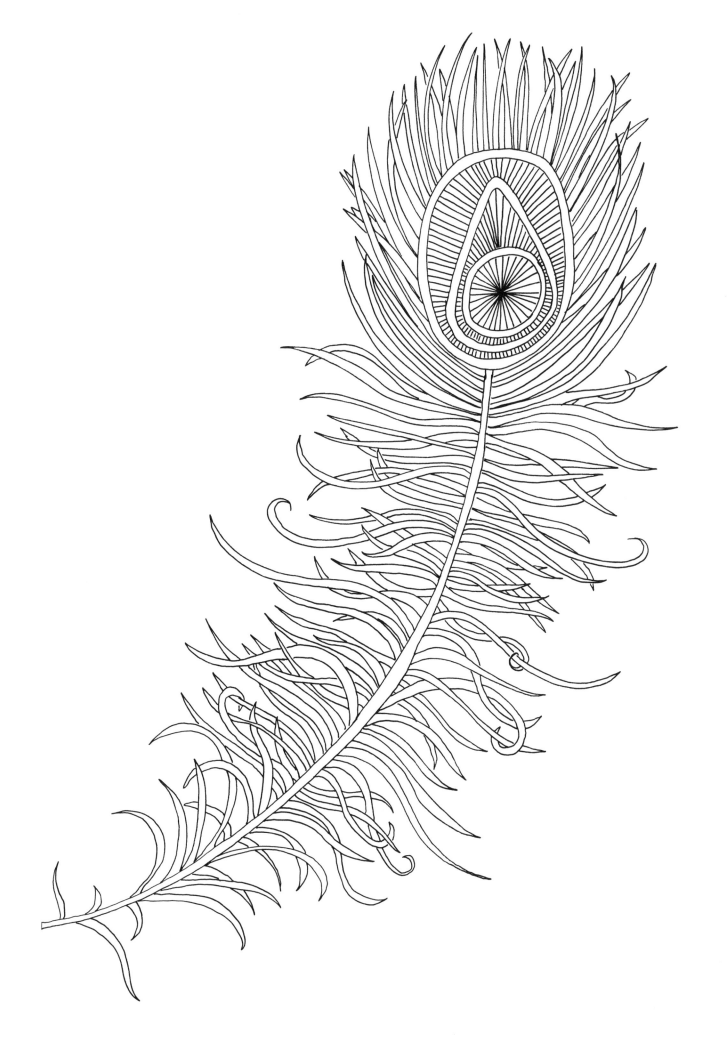

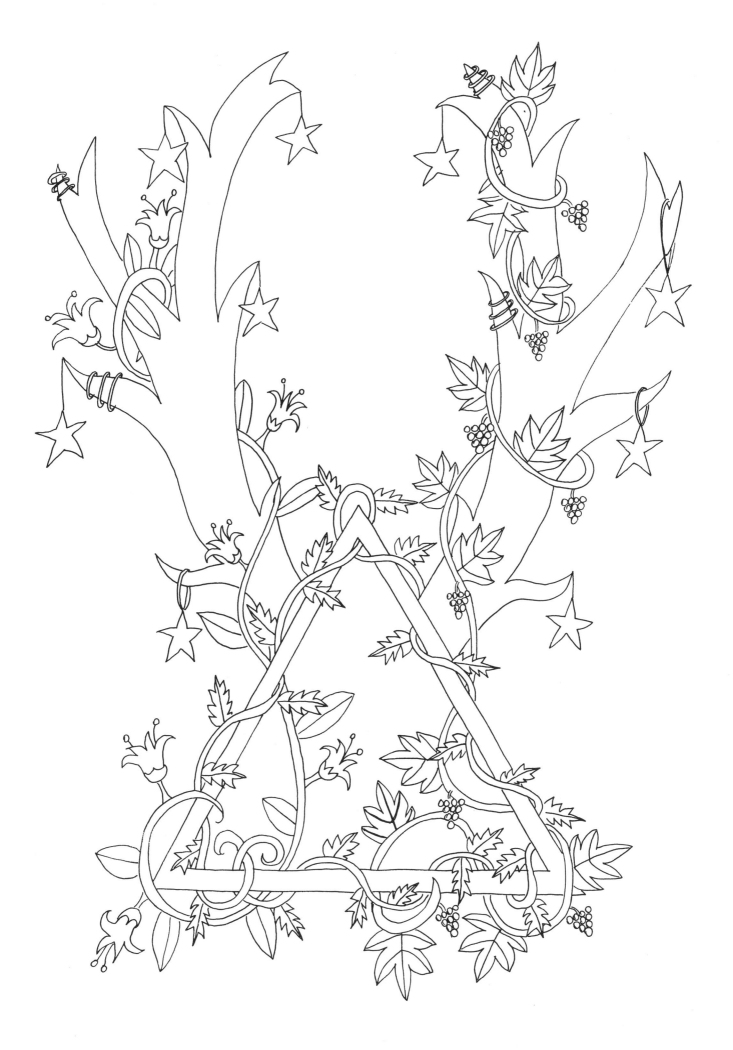

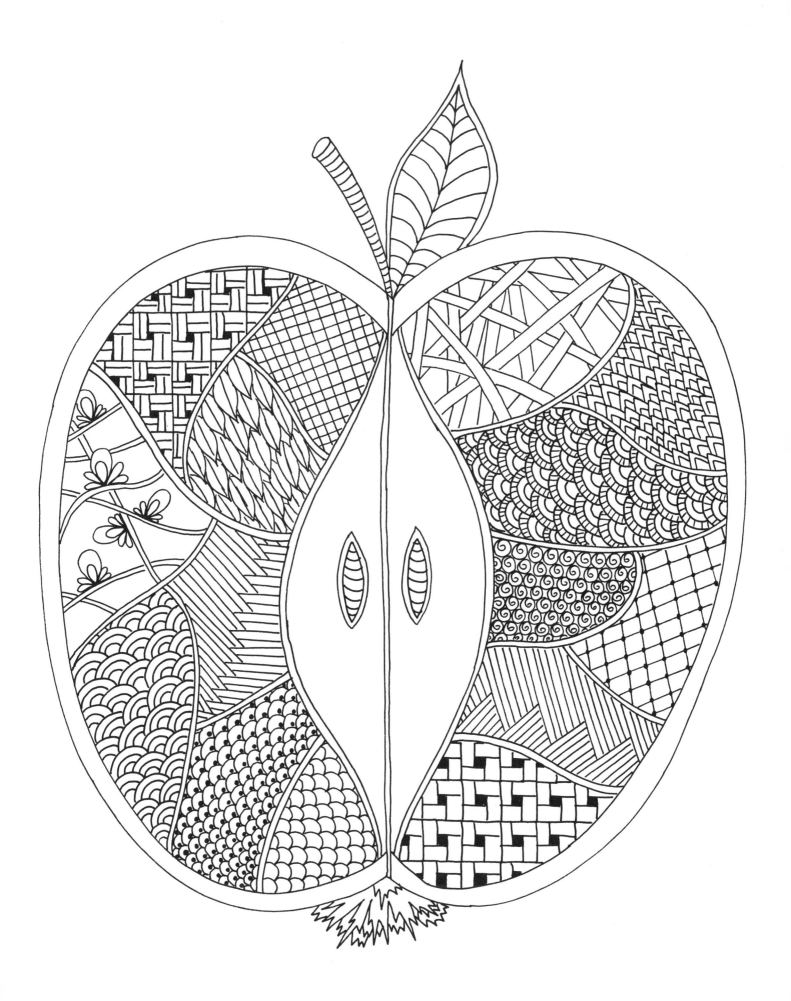

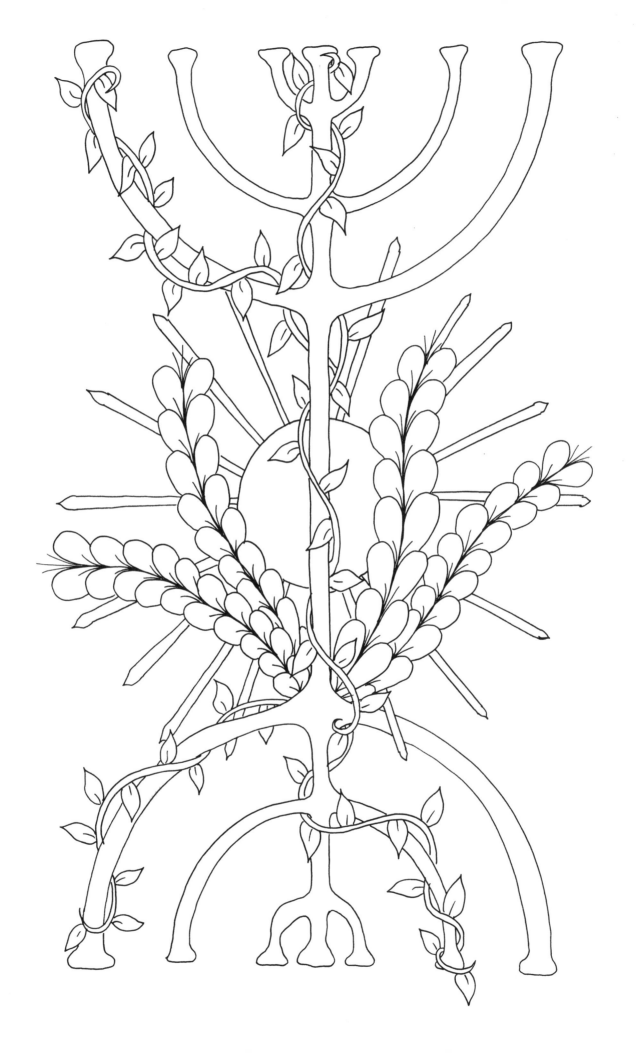

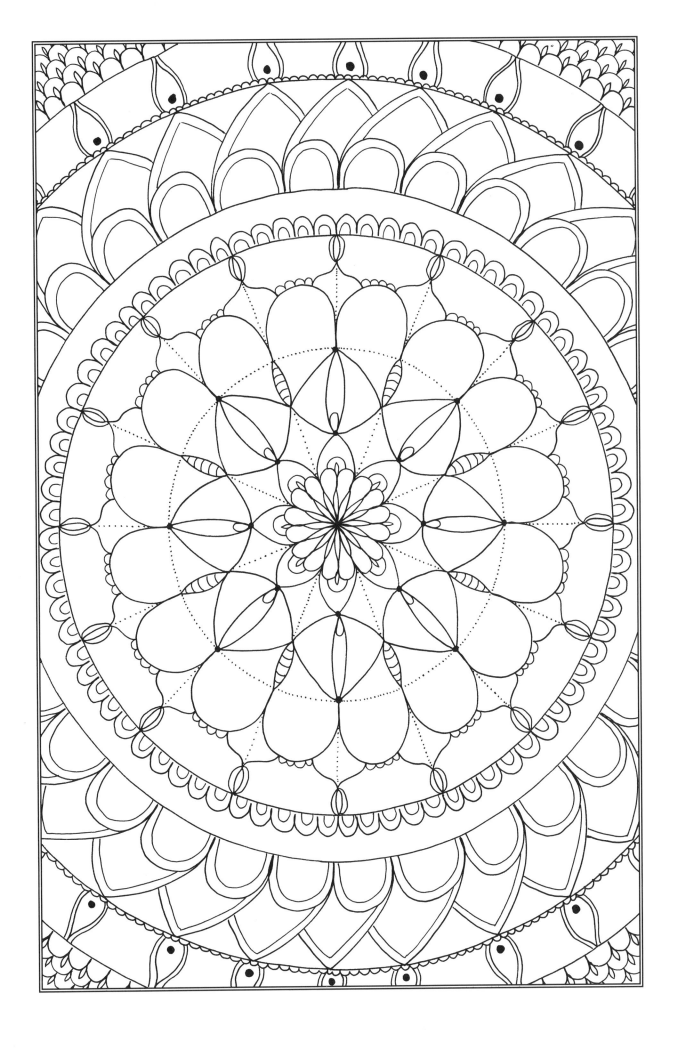

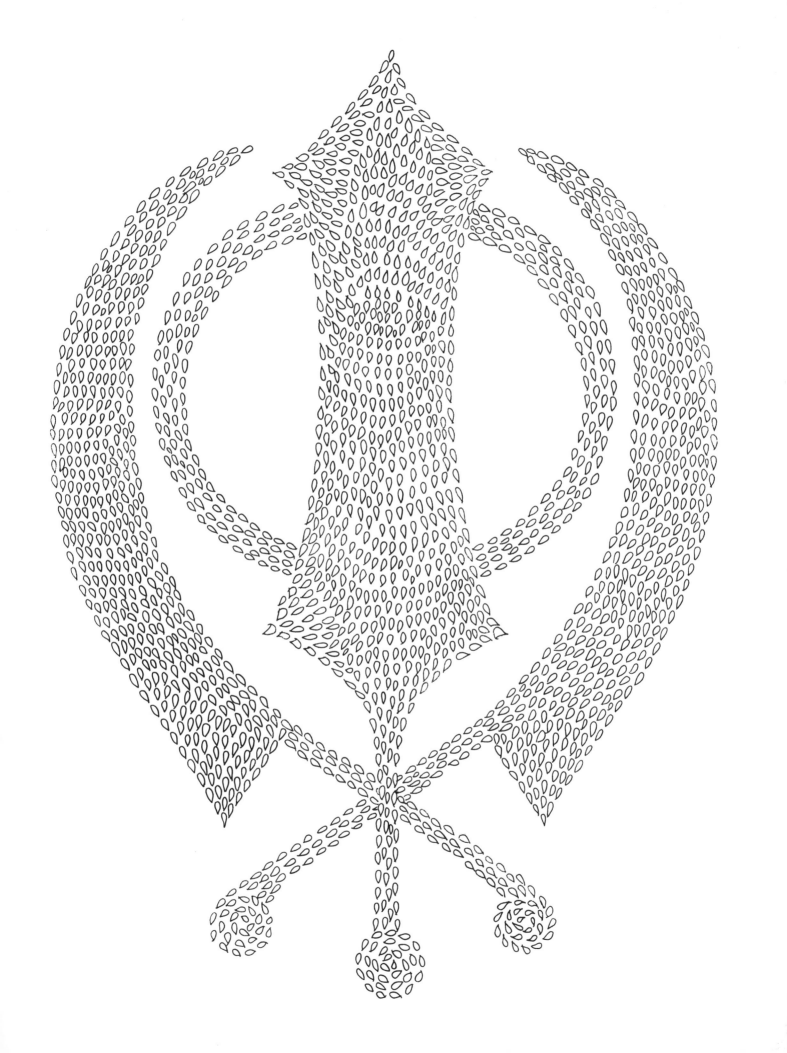

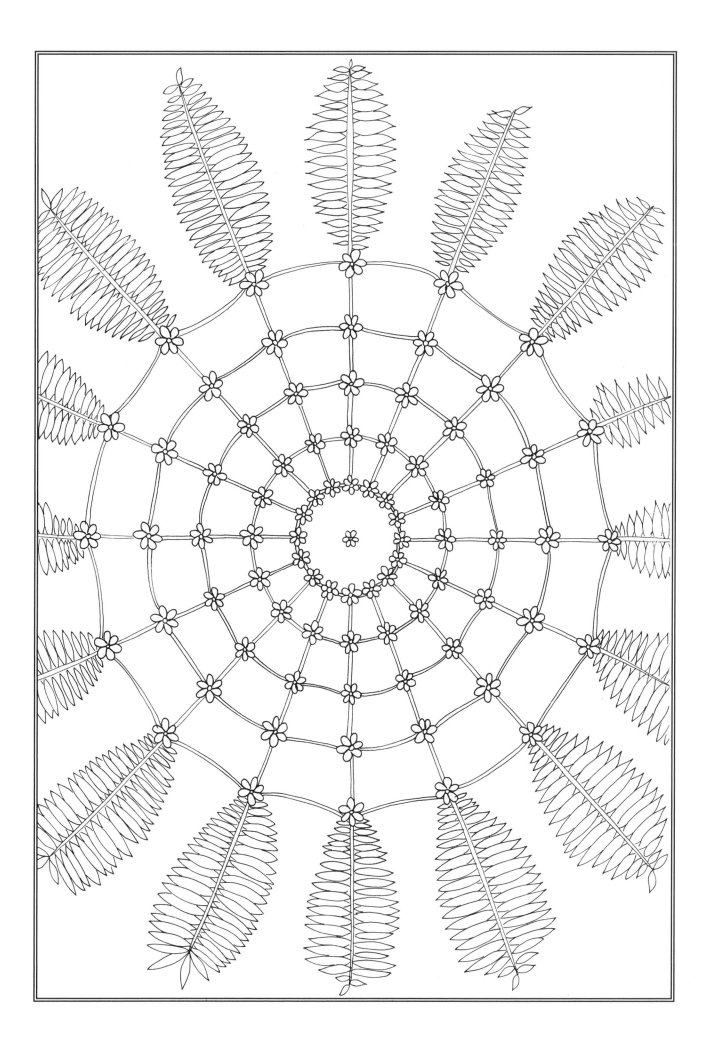

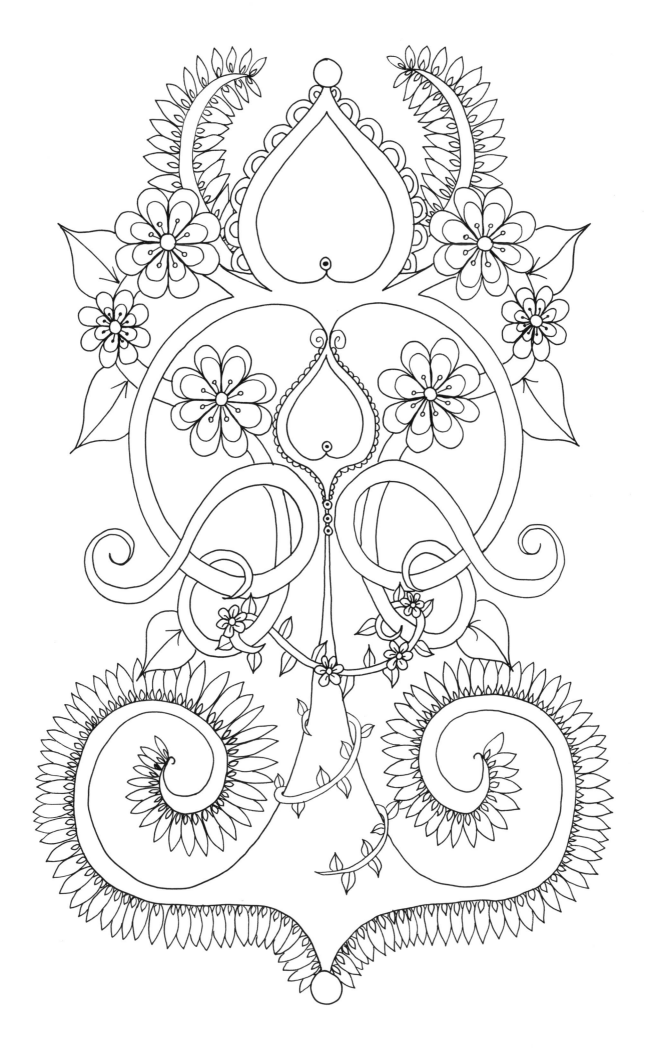

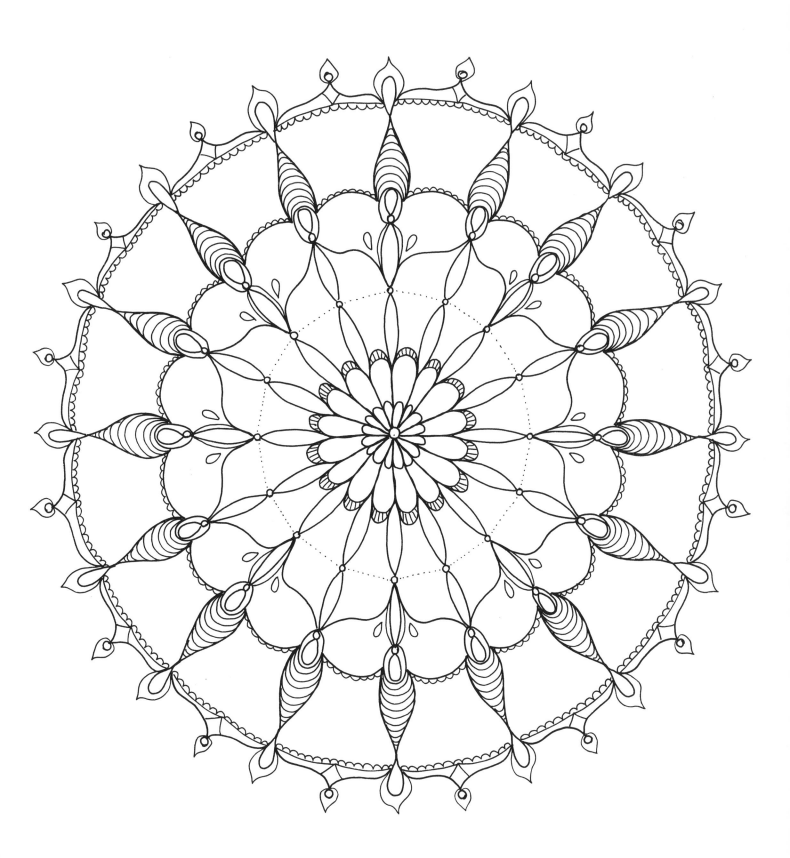

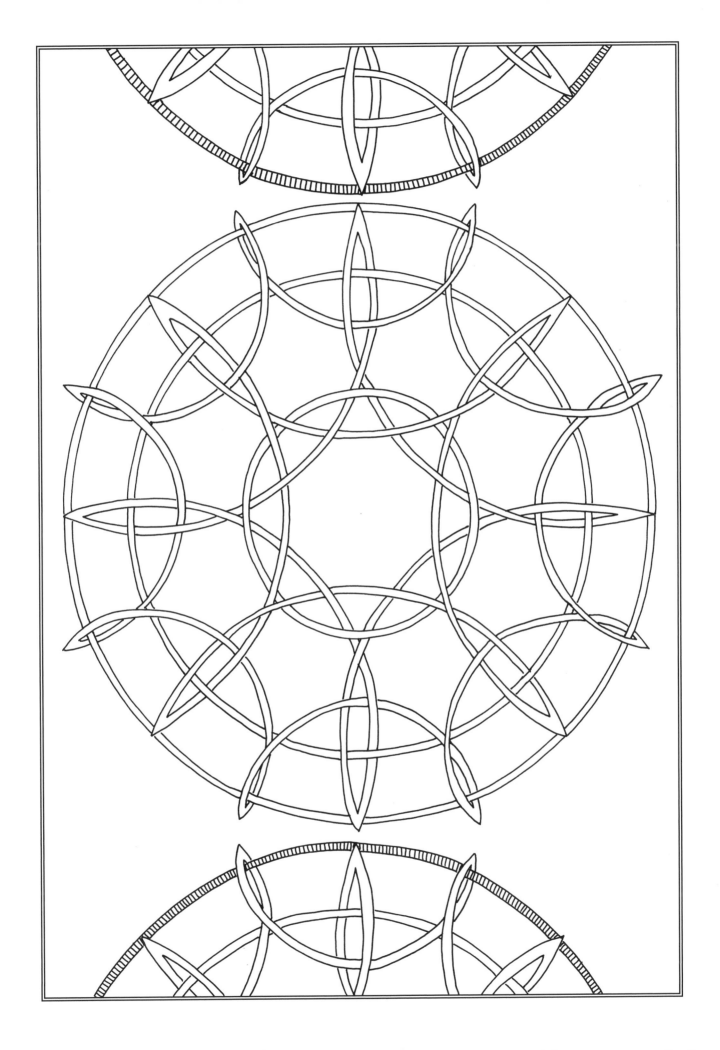

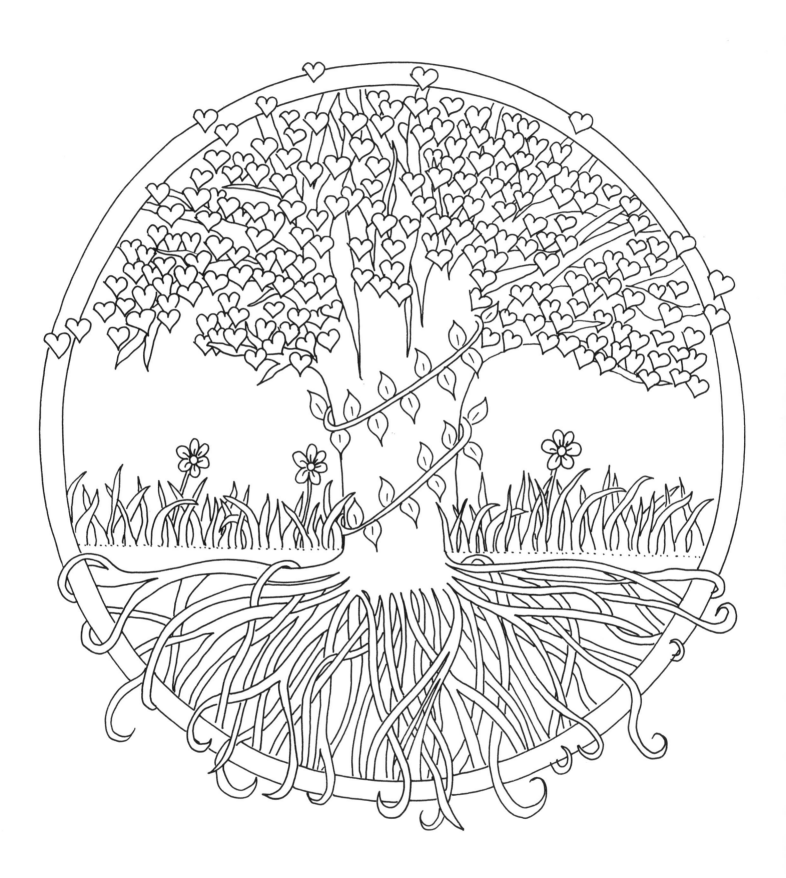

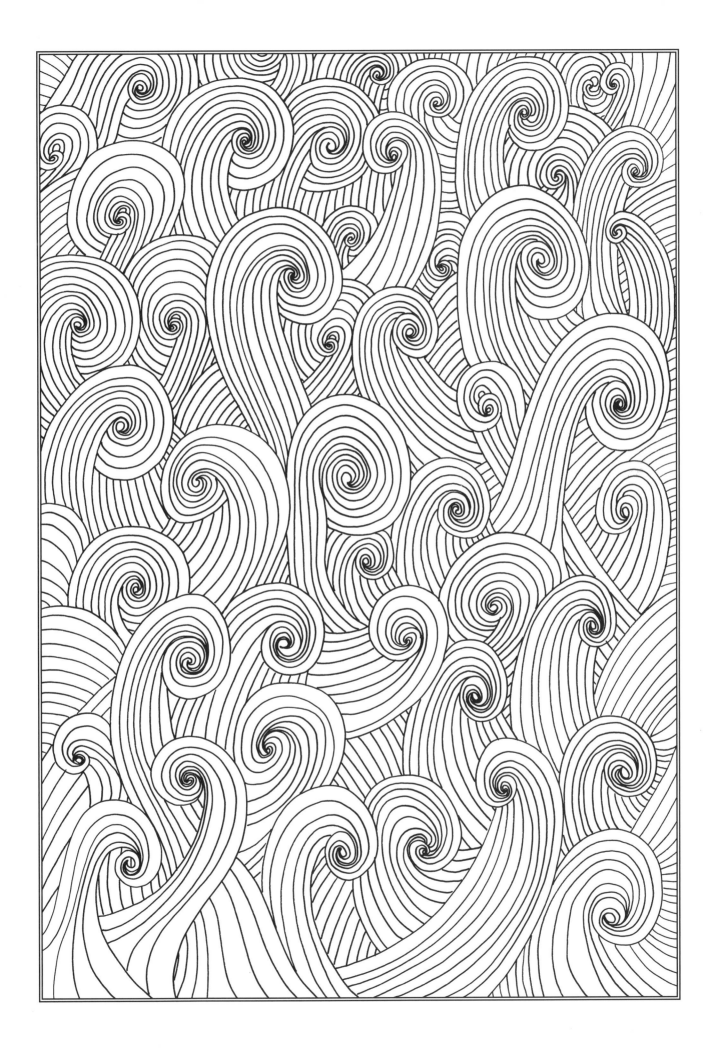

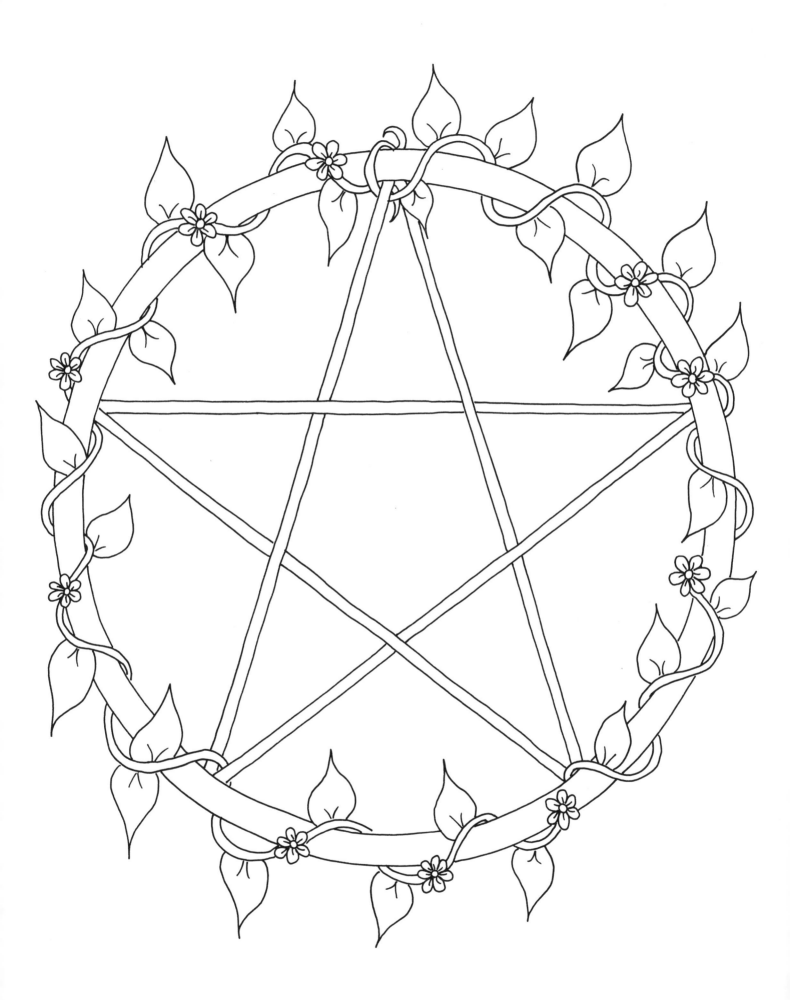

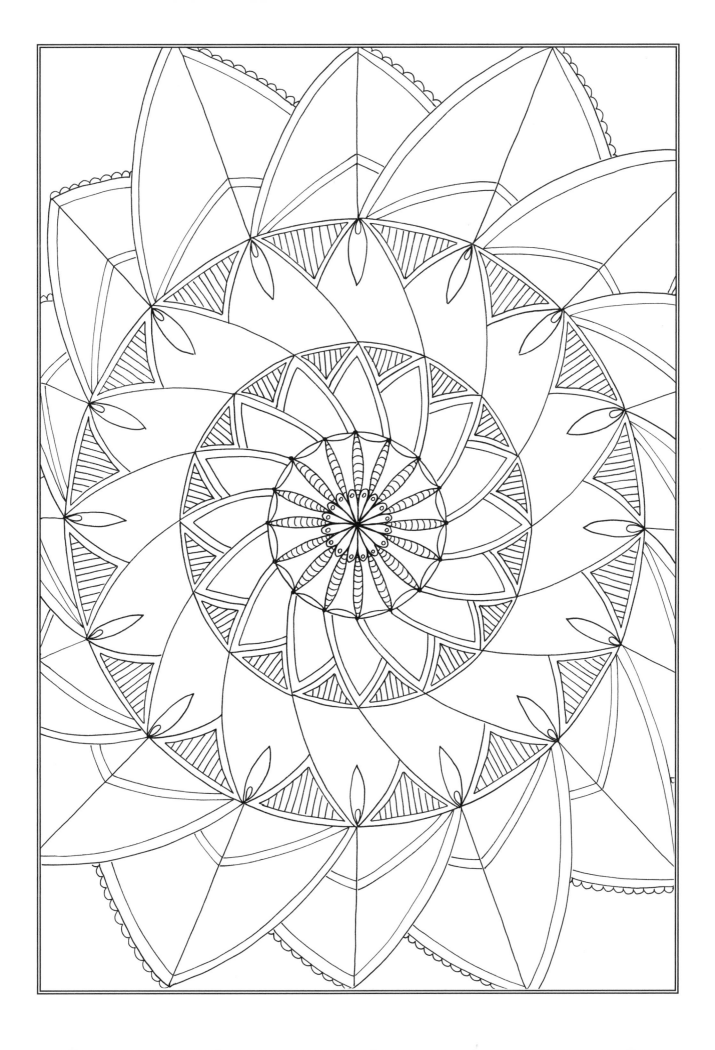

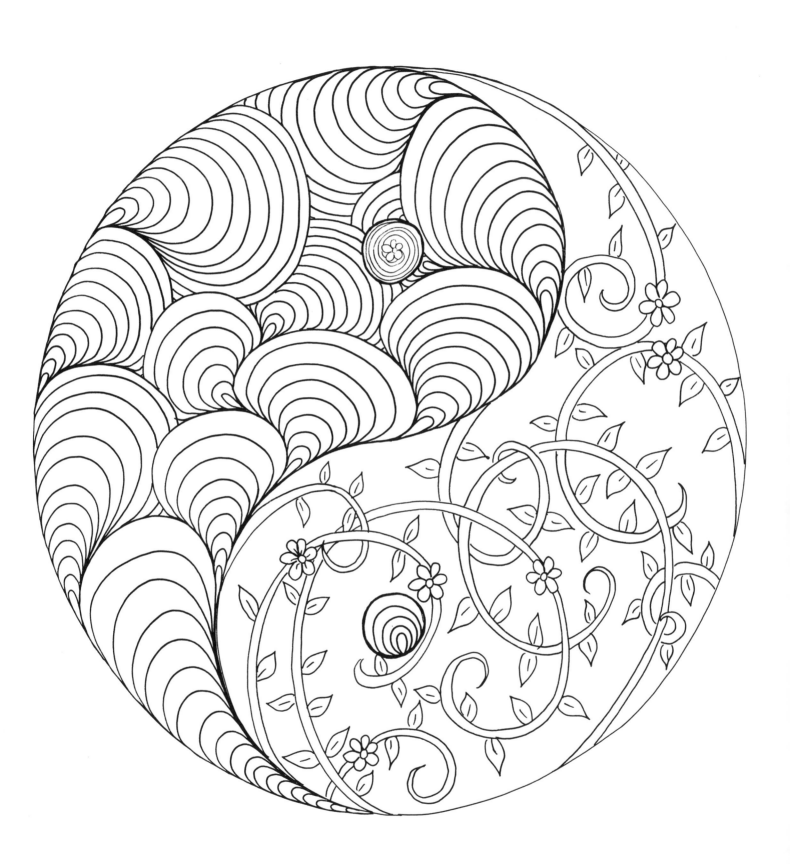

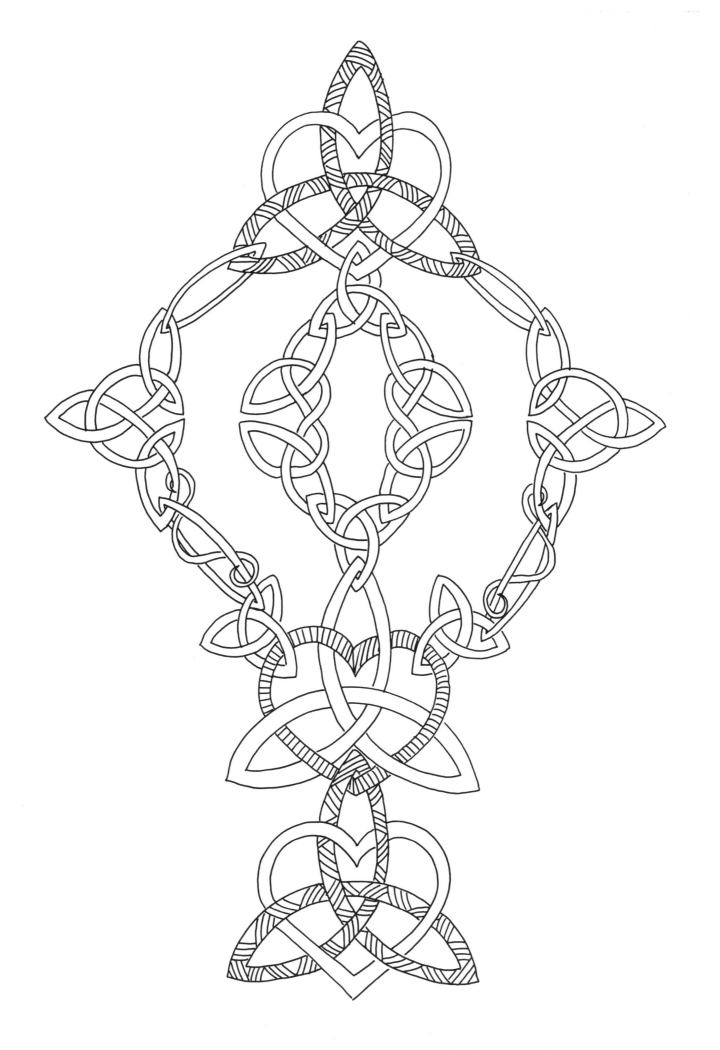

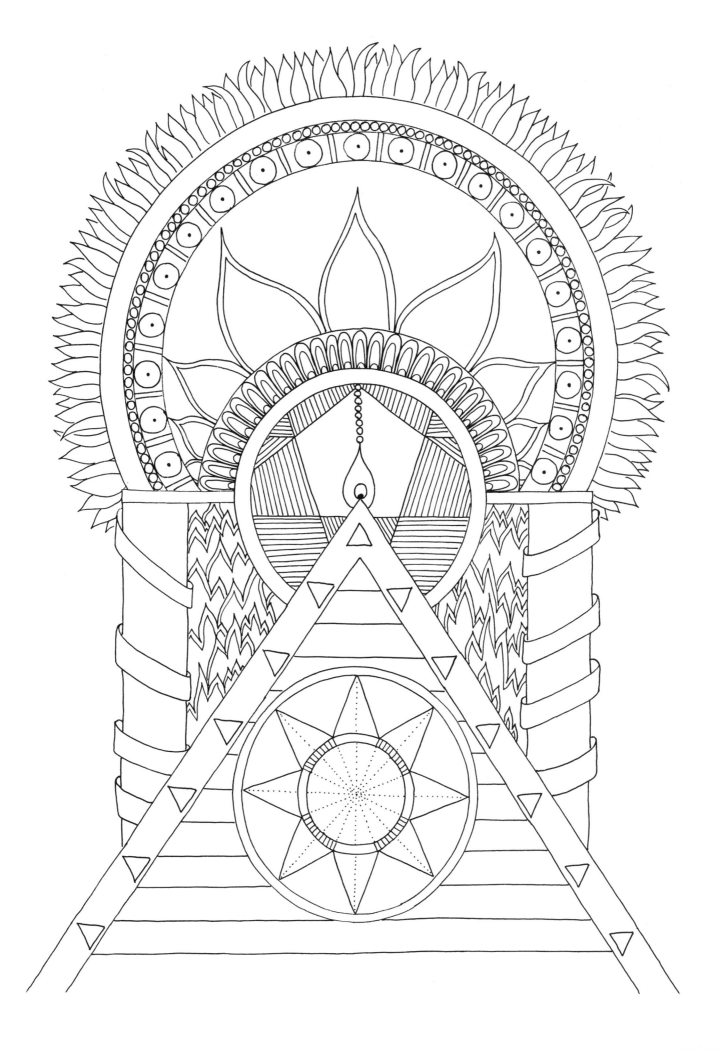

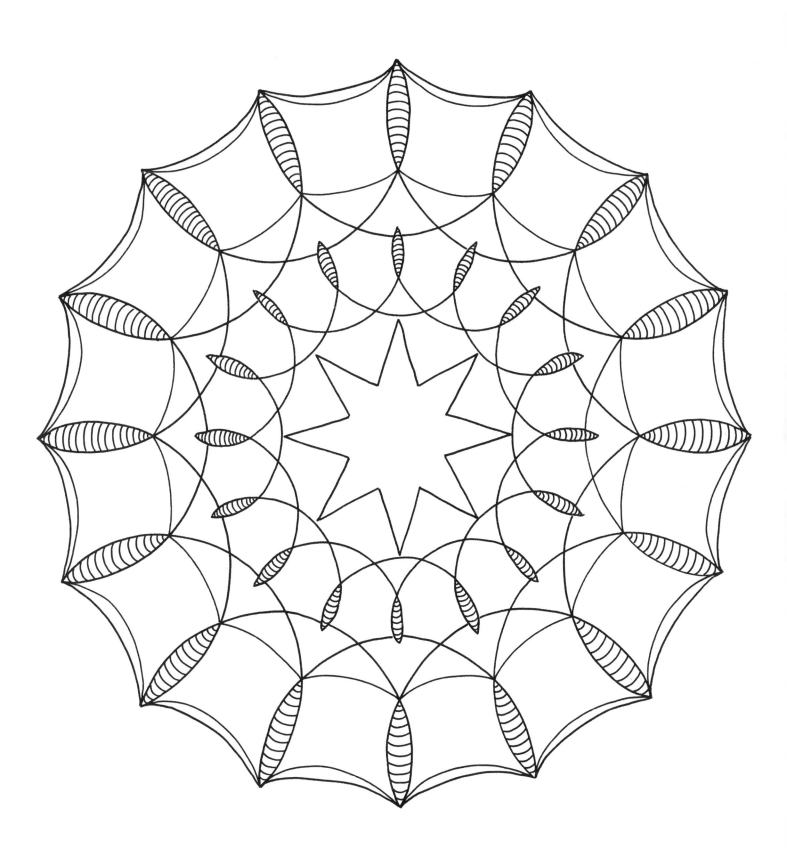

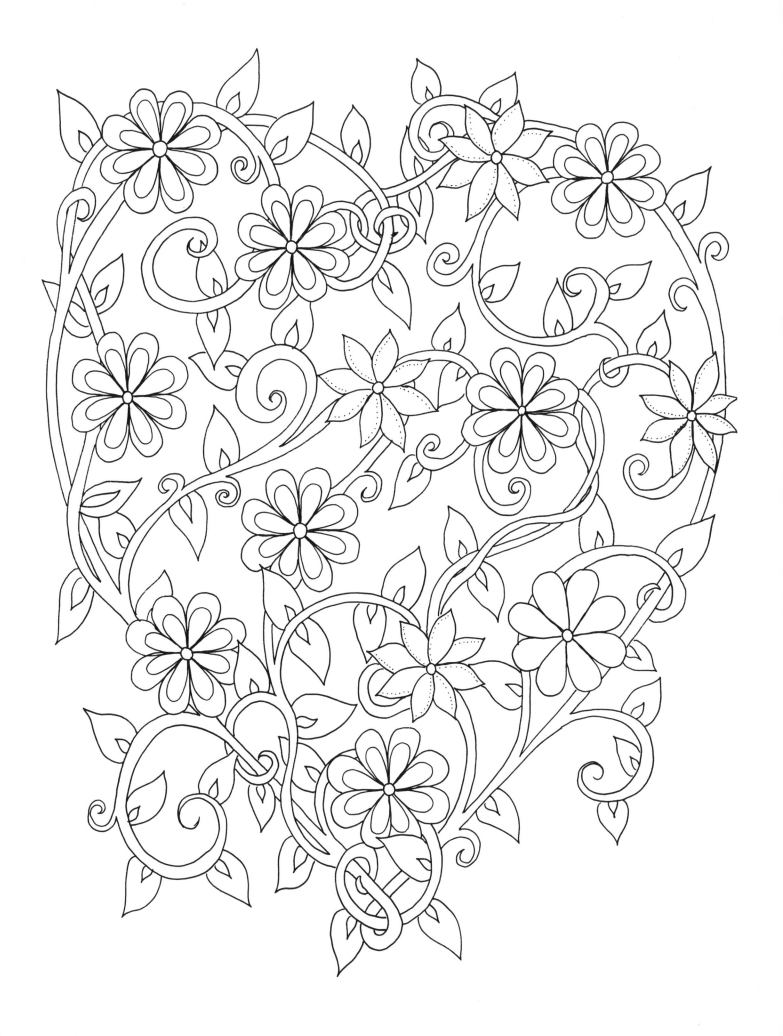

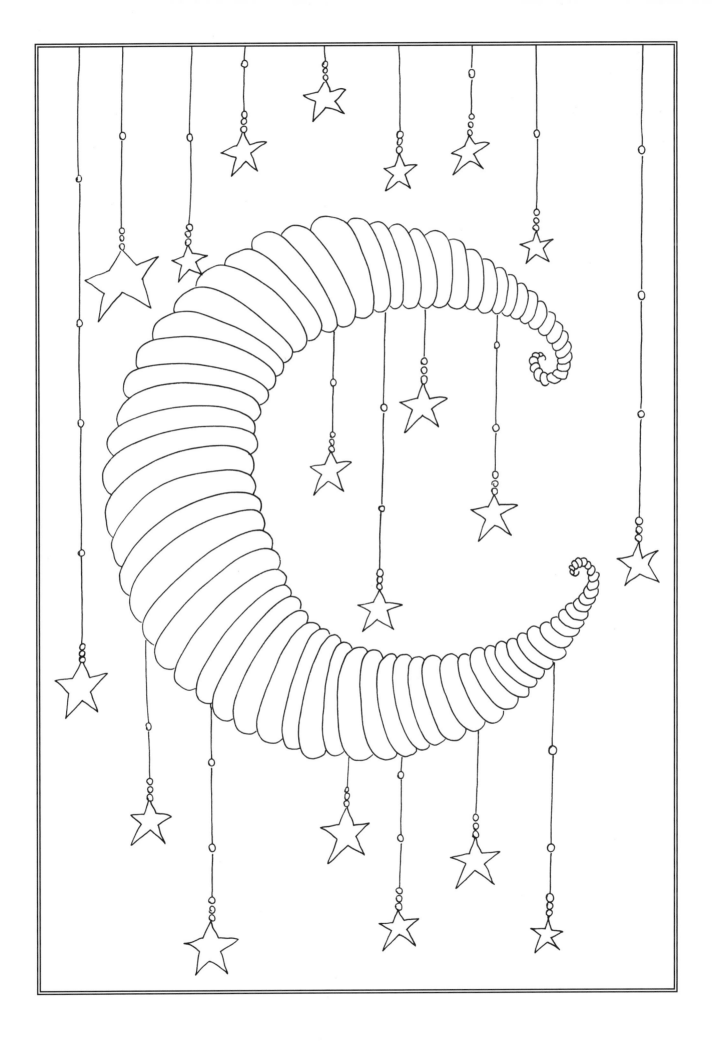

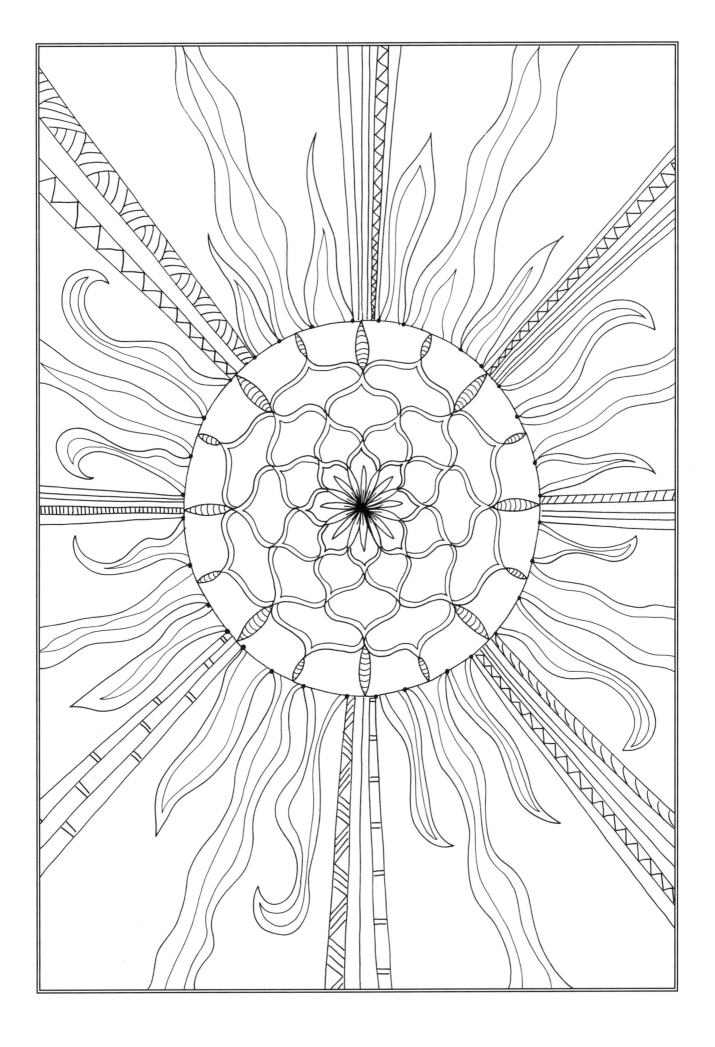

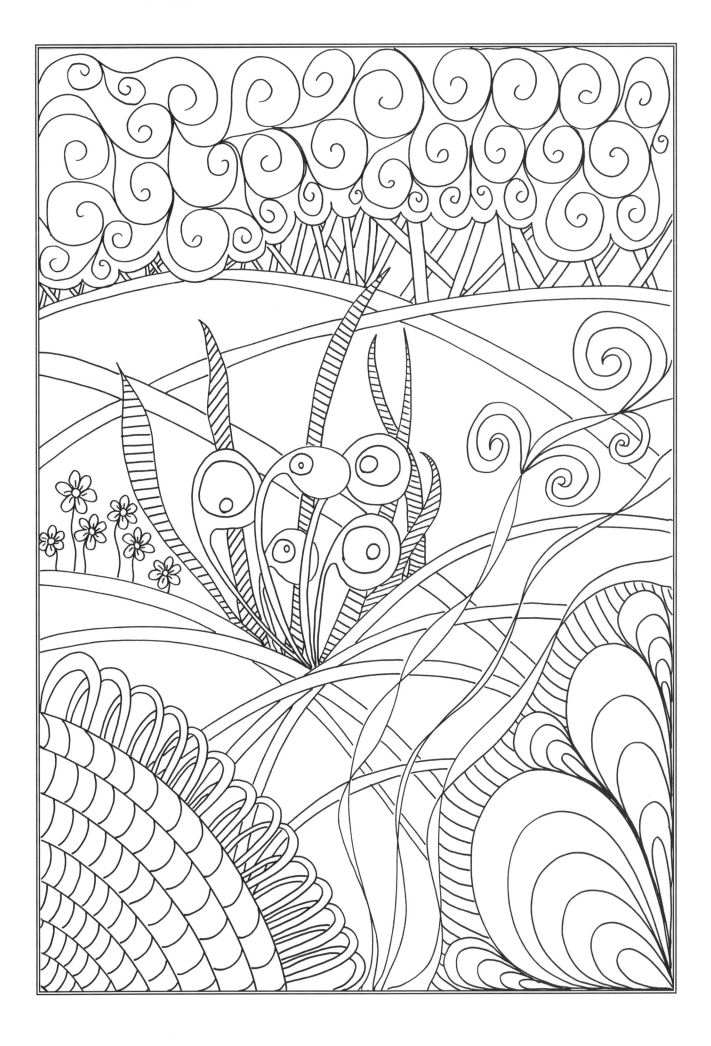

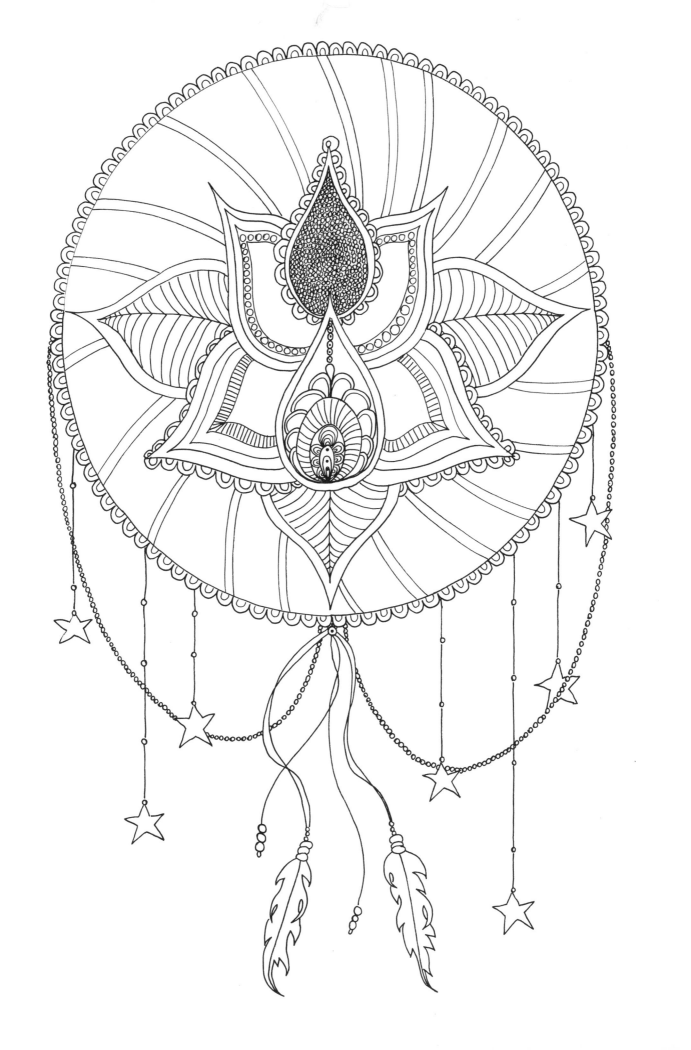

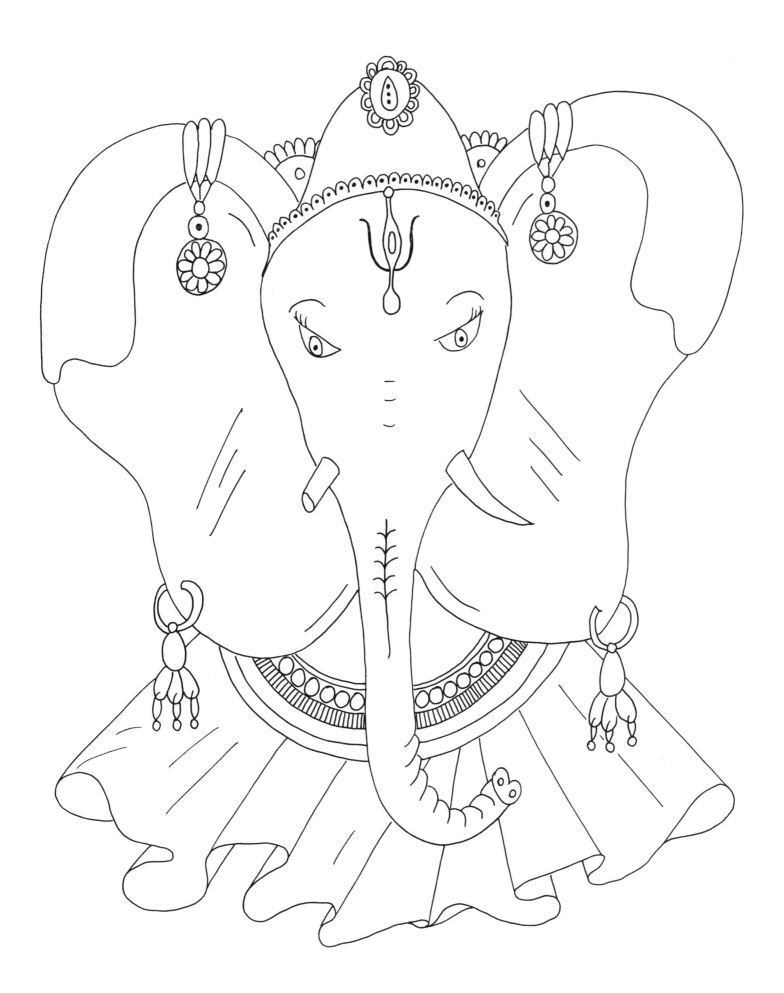

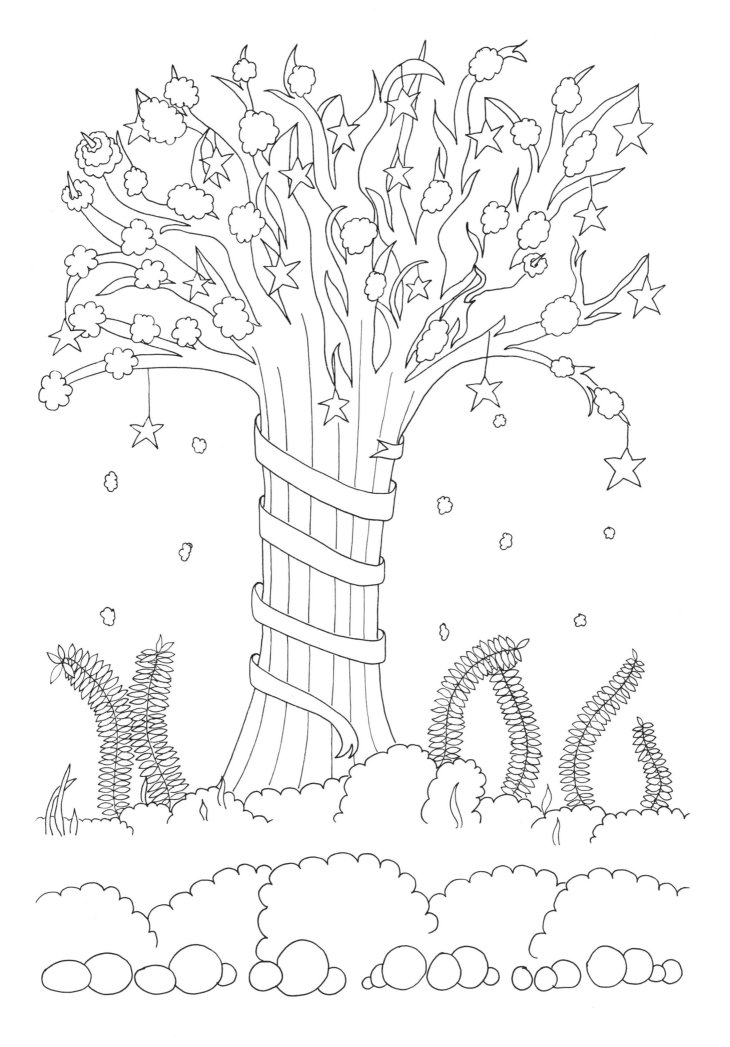

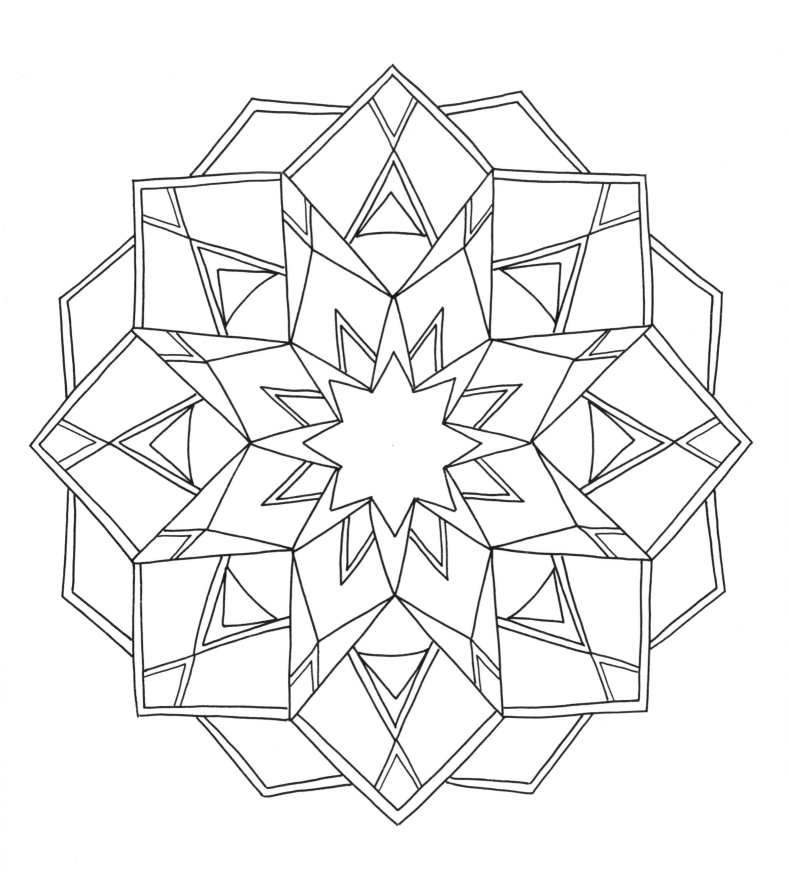

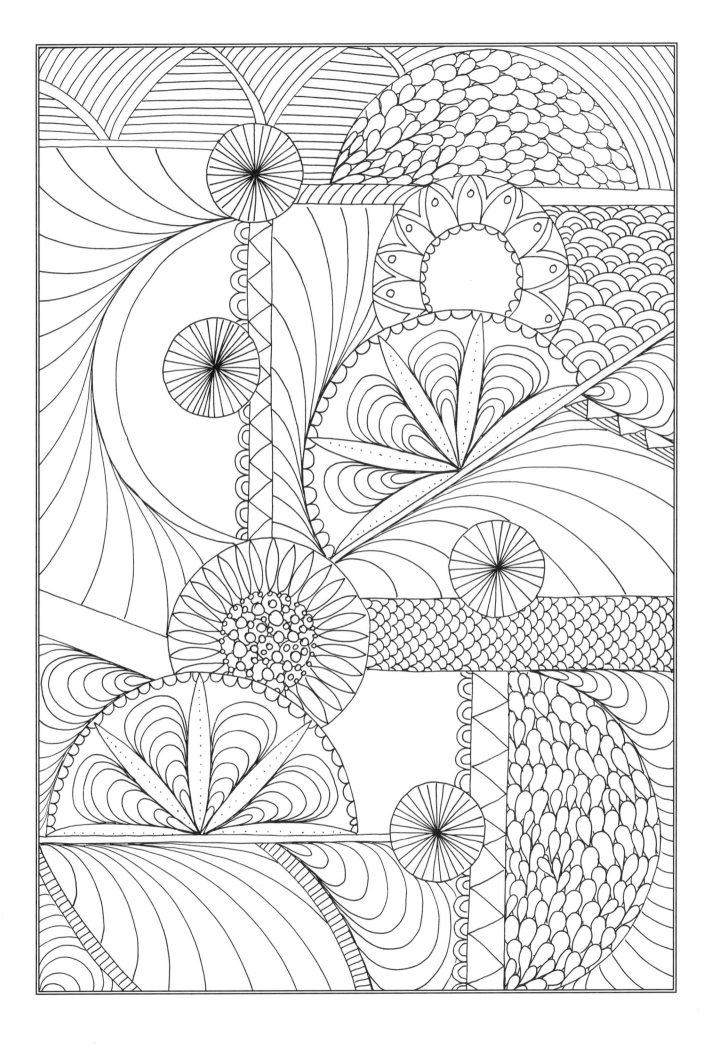

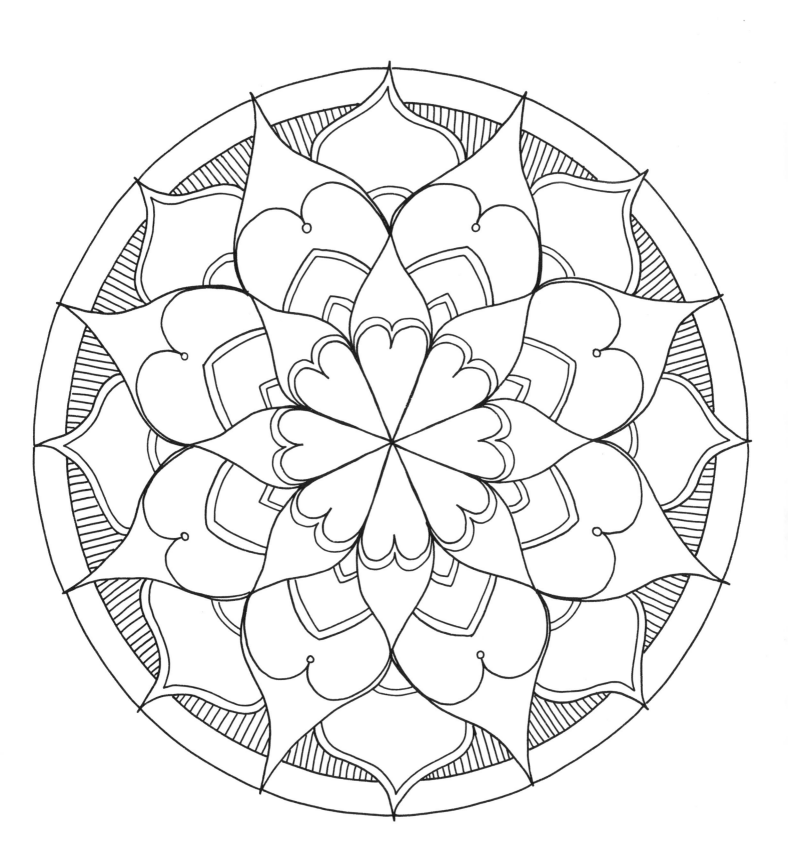